BIOLOGY
PROJECTS FOR YOUNG SCIENTISTS

SALVATORE TOCCI

BIOLOGY
PROJECTS FOR
YOUNG SCIENTISTS

FINES ARE CHARGED

A GROLIER COMPANY

PROJECTS FOR YOUNG SCIENTISTS
FRANKLIN WATTS I 1987
NEW YORK I LONDON I TORONTO I SYDNEY

Cover photograph courtesy of Bio-Tec Images,
George D. Lepp, photographer.

All photographs courtesy of Salvatore Tocci except the following:
Photo Researchers, Inc.: pp. 14 (Hugh Spencer, National Audubon
Society), 55 (Biophoto Associates), 90 (CBS/Science Source); Scripps
Institution of Oceanography: p. 26; Taurus Photos: p. 49 (Martin M.
Rotker); Carolina Biological Supply Company: pp. 64, 97, 100.

Library of Congress Cataloging-in-Publication Data

Tocci, Salvatore.
Biology projects for young scientists.

(Projects for young scientists)
Bibliography: p.
Includes index.
Summary: A collection of biological science projects which
demonstrate concepts and aspects of photosynthesis, genetics,
plant and animal development, cell structure, and biochemistry.
1. Biology—Experiments—Juvenile literature.
(1. Biology—Experiments. 2. Experiments) I. Title.
II. Series.
QH316.5.T63   1987   574′.072   87-10432
ISBN 0-531-15127-1 (paper ed.) — ISBN 0-531-10429-X (lib. bdg.)

CONTENTS

BIOLOGY
PROJECTS FOR YOUNG SCIENTISTS

To my father and mother,
who encouraged a young scientist

1

WHERE YOUR BIOLOGY
PROJECT CAN LEAD

Reading a biology textbook may give you the idea that scientists know all about living things and can explain how every organism functions. After all, a textbook often just tells you what biologists have discovered or explains how biological principles operate in nature or in the laboratory. But don't be fooled! Biology still has many areas to explore and questions to answer. In fact, every biologist could write more about what we *don't* know than what we *do* know. Here's your chance to add to our knowledge by conducting a biology project.

This book contains ideas for biology projects that can be done either in school or at home. To help you get started, procedures are explained briefly for many of the projects described in each chapter. But this is not a book about laboratory techniques. For some projects, you may have to check additional resources for information on specific methods or procedures.

Begin by checking the references listed in the bibliography. As you read through this book, you will come across places where you are specifically asked to check the bibliography. Don't limit yourself to the references listed there. A good biologist reads as much as possible about his or her field. Once you have chosen a topic for your project, the first thing to do is to read as much as you can about your subject. Use your school's library. Read not only books, but scientific magazines and professional journals. Check with your librarian for specific titles. Also speak to the librarian at a local college for resources not available at your school.

THE SCIENTIFIC METHOD

Once you feel knowledgeable about your topic, begin planning your experiments. Biologists often work by following what is known as the scientific method. From reading and observing, biologists may raise a question or see a problem. To get an answer or find a solution, they start by forming a hypothesis. This is simply an educated guess, suggesting a possible answer to the question being investigated. Biologists next work out the detailed steps to follow in conducting their experiments. One thing they are always careful to include is a control whenever necessary.

A control is simply a standard of comparison. Biologists will set up two groups, identical in all respects but one. One group is subjected to the factor being investigated; the other group is not. For example, if you wished to test the effects of radiation on the growth of earthworms, you would expose some worms to X-rays. These make up the experimental group. You would keep other worms in identical physical surroundings, feed them the same way, and treat them exactly alike, but would not expose them to any radiation. These make up the control group. If the radiation had any effect, you should observe a noticeable difference between the experimental and control groups.

Next, biologists collect data. Record everything you observe while conducting your project. Don't overlook anything. A chance discovery or casual observation may lead to some surprise finding. Record your data in a neat and organized manner in a book used only for your project. You may record your observations as notes, drawings, photographs, or in the form of numerical data. Make graphs and tables to organize your numerical data.

A microcomputer may be useful in organizing your data. In fact, you could use a microcomputer as part of your project in other ways. If you enjoy working with computers, you may want to develop a program to simulate a real-life situation. For example, you may find it difficult, if not impossible, to conduct a project investigating the pattern of evolution in some large organism. But with a computer, you might be able to create a simulation to mimic the real world and predict what might happen. As you read this book, see where a microcomputer might be helpful and perhaps add to the scientific nature of your project.

In the final step of the scientific method, biologists examine their data to see if they can reach some conclusion. This is where biologists try to explain their results, arriving at conclusions clearly stated and supported by the data. There should be no doubt that every conclusion is justified by the data collected. Therefore, experiments are always repeated to obtain sufficient data before reaching any conclusions.

SAFETY ADVICE

All projects should be done under supervision, either from a parent, teacher, or scientist. The more complicated the project, the more knowledge you will need about proper procedures and safety factors. Just talk over all the safety aspects with the person helping with your project. If any doubt arises, seek advice from someone knowledgeable about the topic you are investigating.

No matter what type of project you undertake, always follow safety guidelines. In most cases, this simply means using common sense: Don't eat or drink from laboratory equipment, don't taste any chemicals, and keep your work area as clean and organized as possible.

In addition, you should be aware of other rules: Wear protective eye goggles when working with chemicals;

handle toxic or flammable substances with care; read instructions carefully before using any specialized equipment; report any dangerous situations or injuries to your teacher or parent; never perform an experiment without noting precautions that should be taken; and always handle live animals in a humane manner. This last rule applies especially to vertebrates—animals with backbones—like fish, amphibians, reptiles, and mammals. Learn how to handle and treat any animal you use in your project.

SCIENCE FAIRS

Your biology project may lead to your participation in a science fair. This is an ideal opportunity to show off your project and have it judged by professionals, perhaps even a biologist whose interests parallel yours. Science fairs are often sponsored by schools and local organizations. Winning projects selected in these fairs are usually entered in regional, state, or even national competitions. The last step would be the International Science and Engineering Fair, held annually at various locations throughout the country, or the Westinghouse Science Talent Search. If your biology project gets you that far, remember that this book may have been the first step to your success.

2

ORIGIN
OF LIVING THINGS

Most early biologists believed that some animals, such as worms, fish, beetles, and frogs, could originate spontaneously from substances found in mud or dust. This idea of spontaneous generation of life stated that living things could develop quickly from nonliving materials under certain conditions. One biologist working in the 17th century even had a special recipe: Place wheat grains and a sweaty, dirty shirt in an open container in some dark corner, and within 21 days you would have mice!

Even then most biologists did not believe in this recipe, at least for making mice. But the development in the 17th century of better lenses for microscopes led to the discovery of a new world of tiny creatures known as *microorganisms.* With these new lenses, biologists could observe many tiny organisms never seen before. The discovery of these microorganisms supported the belief that such large numbers of tiny creatures could originate only through spontaneous generation.

OBSERVING MICROORGANISMS

With a modern microscope, you can easily explore the world of microorganisms (see Figure 1). Just prepare a

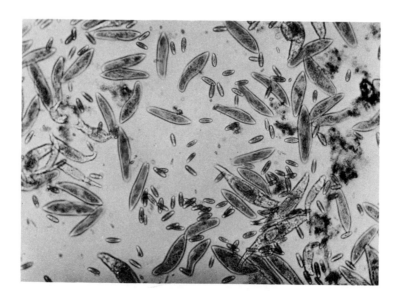

FIGURE 1. AN IMMENSE VARIETY OF LIFE MAY EXIST
IN A SINGLE DROP OF POND WATER. SHOWN HERE ARE
PARAMECIA, ROTIFERS, AND OTHER MICROORGANISMS
(MAGNIFIED 120 TIMES IN THE ORIGINAL PHOTOGRAPH).

wet mount using a drop of water from a pond or rain pud-
dle. Examine your slide closely with the highest-power
objective lens, and you'll discover a variety of microorganisms. Make sketches of what you see.

You can carry out a project describing the microorganisms found in various water samples including drink-
ing fountains, kitchen faucets, mud puddles, melted
snow, or garden hoses. Carefully examine your samples
to see which one contains the most microorganisms and
the greatest variety.

Jot down some general observations for each type of
microorganism you observe, describing its general appearance, any unusual characteristics, and method of
locomotion. Note if the microorganisms share any common features. Observe if they exist as individuals, pairs, or
colonies.

Include measurements with your drawings. The length and width of microorganisms are expressed in micrometers (μ). If your microscope is not equipped with an ocular micrometer, place a millimeter ruler under the low-power objective lens. Determine the diameter of the field of view in millimeters. Convert this to micrometers, keeping in mind that 1 mm equals 1,000 μ.

If your diameter measures 4,000 μ under low power and a microorganism occupies approximately one-quarter of the diameter, you know it measures about 1,000 μ in length. By the way, an inverse relationship exists between the field of view and the power of magnification. If you double the magnification, you decrease the field of view by half. For example, a 4,000-μ diameter under a 10X objective lens becomes a 2,000-μ diameter under a 20X objective.

GETTING MORE MICROORGANISMS

One procedure used by early biologists for getting microorganisms to observe with a microscope involved making an infusion culture by placing some chopped up hay or wheat in water. After a few days, a tremendous number of microorganisms appeared. Many biologists believed these microorganisms developed spontaneously from the hay or wheat.

Prepare your own hay infusion culture. Check samples from various places—near the surface, the bottom, and on the hay or wheat—to see if you find more microorganisms in a particular area. Compare the microorganisms to those you observed in your water samples. Try seeds, leaves, flowers, grasses, weeds, and stems in place of hay to see if microorganisms appear in all types of infusions.

Check your infusions every day to see what happens to the number of microorganisms. You can count the microorganisms with the use of a hemocytometer, a microscope slide ruled with a grid pattern. If you do not have a hemocytometer, count the microorganisms seen under the highest-power objective lens. Do this for ten different areas on the slide and then calculate an average for each day.

Experiment to see how you can affect both the number and variety of microorganisms that appear in your cultures. Investigate how temperature changes affect microorganisms. Does increasing the temperature have the same effect as lowering it by the same amount? Gently boil each culture for 10 minutes. After allowing the culture to cool, prepare a wet mount to see if this treatment killed all the microorganisms. If not, determine the conditions required so that no microorganisms exist in your infusion.

Add small amounts of such household solutions as vinegar, ammonia, orange juice, milk, soda, and honey to your infusions. Which solution is the best inhibitor of microorganism growth? the best promotor?

MAKING IT
EASIER TO SEE
MICROORGANISMS

Observing microorganisms under a microscope is not easy. Since they are so small and often move quickly, you must be patient and observe closely. There are several ways to make your job easier if your project involves observing microorganisms.

One way is to prepare a hanging-drop suspension. Place a drop of your sample on the center of a cover slip. Add a drop or two of water to the edge of the depression of a concave slide. Invert the cover slip and place it over the depression of the slide (see Figure 2).

The drops of water on the edge of the depression will help prevent the cover slip from sliding and also act as a seal so that the hanging drop will not evaporate. The microorganisms will be easier to find in the small drop. In addition, you will be able to observe how they move without being squashed by a cover slip.

Another way to make it easier to observe microorganisms is with an oil immersion lens. This type of lens pro-

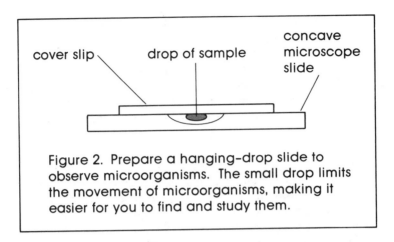

Figure 2. Prepare a hanging-drop slide to observe microorganisms. The small drop limits the movement of microorganisms, making it easier for you to find and study them.

vides a higher magnification. If you use this type of lens, be sure that it is in the oil and not touching the slide. Because of the thickness of the oil, you will need to increase the amount of light striking the slide.

Staining is another method to make the microorganisms more visible. You can use several stains, including methylene blue, crystal violet, safranin O, gentian violet, Congo red, and malachite green. Add a drop of your sample containing microorganisms to a clean glass slide. Let the solution dry. Quickly pass the slide, face up, through a Bunsen burner flame three times. The heat will kill and fix the microorganisms to the slide. Add the stain, wash off any excess with water, and allow the slide to dry thoroughly. Be careful since the dye can also stain your hands, clothes, and work area. Examine your stained specimens under the highest-power objective lens. You do not need a cover slip.

With some microorganisms, especially bacteria, it is easier to see them by staining the background and leaving the organisms unstained. This procedure is called negative staining. Negative staining can also help you determine the shape and arrangement of bacteria. Bacteria can have the shape of rods, spheres, or spirals and can be arranged in chains, pairs, or colonies.

To prepare a negative stain, place a drop of Congo red in the center of a clean slide. Add a drop of your water sample or infusion culture to the stain. Gently mix the stain and culture sample. After mounting the cover slip, observe the slide under the highest power or oil immersion lens. The bacteria will appear transparent, while the surrounding areas will be a dark red.

BACTERIA

Bacteria can be used for many different types of projects. If you want to work with them, you won't have to look very far to find them since no group of organisms, with the possible exception of the insects, is as widespread. Bacteria live in a variety of environments, from hot sulfur springs to the ice packs of the polar regions. You cannot name an area on earth where you could not find bacteria.

To get the most bacteria in the shortest possible time, you should use special culture media. These media can include natural ingredients (blood, milk, eggs, animal tissues), synthetic combinations (including a variety of chemicals), and special preparations (materials processed from plants and animals). One of the most commonly used media is known as nutrient broth.

Nutrient broth includes a chemical ingredient (peptone) and beef extract added to distilled water. You can purchase peptone or even the nutrient broth from a scientific supply company.

If you want to make your own broth, prepare the beef extract by boiling lean beef in water until you get a thick paste. Nutrient broth is made by dissolving 5 g of peptone and 3 g of beef extract in 1 liter of distilled water. The mixture is heated at 60°C until the ingredients are dissolved.

To prevent any unwanted growth of microorganisms in the broth, seal the solution with cotton and sterilize it in a pressure cooker for 25 minutes (see Figure 3). Store the sterilized broth in a refrigerator until needed. Also sterilize all glassware.

FIGURE 3. STERILIZE GLASSWARE AND SOLUTIONS
IN A HOUSEHOLD PRESSURE COOKER.

One project you can do with the nutrient broth involves collecting bacteria from the air. Pour 100 ml of the nutrient broth into a sterile 250-ml flask. Expose the flask to the air for 10 minutes, then stopper the opening with cotton. After a few days, observe the broth. Describe what you see. **Be careful not to spill or touch the broth since some of the bacteria growing in the flask may be pathogenic (disease-causing). When you are finished with any culture, sterilize the flask to kill the bacteria before pouring the solution down a drain.**

Experiment by varying the amounts of peptone and beef extract to see which combination provides the best environment for bacterial growth. See what happens if you add small amounts of sugar, such as glucose or lactose. Expose your flasks to the air in different locations to see which area contains the most bacteria.

One way to measure the amount of bacteria growing in a culture involves using a spectrophotometer. When light strikes a solution containing bacteria, part is reflected, part is scattered at different angles, and part continues to be transmitted in its original direction. A spectrophotometer measures the amount of this transmitted light. The more bacteria, the less light transmitted. With a spectrophotometer, you can plot bacterial growth over a period of time. Experiment with different media to see which is best for growing bacteria.

GROWING BACTERIA
ON SOMETHING SOLID

Working with bacteria can sometimes be easier if you have a solid surface on which they can grow. The most commonly used solid media is agar, a chemical obtained from seaweed. Agar is a liquid at high temperatures but solidifies below 42°C. Nutrient agar contains food materials, salts, minerals, and all the other chemicals needed to provide an ideal environment for bacterial growth.

Just add 15 g of agar, which you can obtain from a scientific supply company, to 1 liter of nutrient broth to make nutrient agar. You can buy nutrient agar as a powder, or ready to use in either test tubes or petri dishes.

If you prepare your own nutrient agar test tubes and petri dishes, you must first sterilize the agar and glassware. Wipe your work surface area with alcohol. Pass the neck of the flask containing the sterilized agar through the flame from a Bunsen burner before pouring it into the test tube or petri dish. Seal the test tubes with sterile cotton. Once the agar solidifies, refrigerate the materials until you are ready to use them.

You can use petri dishes containing nutrient agar to collect bacteria and other microorganisms from some surface. Rub a sterile cotton swab over the surface of your desk and then gently streak the swab over the surface of the agar. Do not press too hard or you'll break the agar. Turn the dish upside down so that any water which condenses can evaporate and not drop on the agar to contaminate it. After a few days, check the dish for any microorganisms. If you have an incubator, set the temperature to 27°C for the bacteria to grow more quickly.

Besides your desk, you can check different areas for bacteria: your locker, the nurse's office, the cafeteria table, various places in your home, or different parts of your body. Record the location on the petri dish with a grease pencil or waterproof marker.

The bacteria will grow in roughly circular shapes (see Figure 4). Each circle is called a colony, which represents millions of bacteria all derived from a single cell that grew and reproduced in the spot. Compare your colonies. Describe any differences in terms of size, shape, and color. Why do you get more colonies from certain areas?

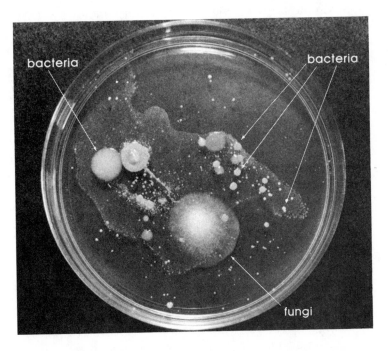

FIGURE 4. BACTERIA GROW IN ROUGHLY CIRCULAR SHAPES, WHILE FUNGI APPEAR AS FINE STRANDS ON NUTRIENT AGAR.

Some of the colonies may look like fine strands; these are fungi.

Whatever grows, don't open your dishes. Observe the colonies with a hand lens or dissecting microscope through the cover of the dish. Remember not to touch any colony since it may be pathogenic.

CHANGING THE BACTERIAL ENVIRONMENT

Now that you know how to culture bacteria on agar plates, you can carry out a project to see how changes in their environment affect their growth.

After you have spread the bacteria over the surface of the agar, spray the plates with mouthwashes, disinfectants, or household cleaning solutions. Add different antibiotics in the form of disks available from scientific supply companies, or try different chemicals such as ethanol, nicotine, caffeine, and aspirin powder. Check with someone for special precautions you must follow if you work with a chemical additive.

Here are more project ideas.

- Salt is sometimes added to foods to prevent bacterial growth. In the presence of salt, bacterial cells will lose water, shrink, and eventually die. Prepare sterilized solutions of different salt concentrations and spread a small amount over the agar. Determine which is most effective in preventing bacterial growth.
- Ultraviolet light is used to sterilize the air in such places as hospitals, laboratories, restaurants, and dairy plants. If you have an ultraviolet light source, experiment with different exposure times. Keep in mind that practically anything, including plastic, glass, and paper, will stop ultraviolet light. However, do not look into the ultraviolet light since it can damage your eyes.
- Radiation is sometimes used to kill cells. Contact your local hospital to see if you can test the

effects of low levels of radiation on the growth of bacteria. Plot the number of colonies growing on agar dishes versus the amount of radiation.

- Perhaps you might be interested in testing the effects of loud music, ultrasonic vibrations, different colored lights, or pungent odors on bacterial growth. Some of these environmental factors have been shown to affect humans. You may turn up some interesting results on bacteria!

PURE STRAINS OF BACTERIA

Rather than using a mixture of different types of bacteria to study the effects of environmental changes, you may want a pure culture consisting of only one type of bacteria. In this way, your project can be more specific by testing how ultraviolet light or radiation affects a particular type of bacteria.

You can purchase pure strains of bacteria, or you can isolate a pure strain from a mixed culture by preparing a streak plate. Divide a nutrient agar plate into four parts. Sterilize an inoculating loop by passing it through a flame. Allow it to cool and then collect a loop of a mixed bacterial culture, perhaps from one of your petri dishes.

Use a back and forth streaking motion to streak the bacteria onto one area of the sterile agar dish. Sterilize the loop again and then pick up some bacteria from the first area. Use these bacteria to streak a second area on the dish. Repeat this procedure for the third and fourth areas on the dish (see Figure 5).

After 24 to 48 hours, check the third and fourth areas for a pure culture by seeing if only one type of bacterial colony is growing in that location. If not, repeat the procedure using the bacteria from your first streak plate.

One project where a pure culture of bacteria would be most helpful is a study of the effects of low temperatures on living cells. Our understanding in this area is still very limited. Yet knowledge gained from this project would have application in such areas as space travel (suspended animation), medicine (preserving organs for

Figure 5. Prepare a streak plate to isolate a pure culture of bacteria. Streak the bacteria on the agar surface, alternating the "S" pattern for each quadrant of the dish.

transplants), and genetics (freezing sperm, eggs, and embryos).

Design an experiment to test the effects of freezing temperatures on bacteria. Use a mixture of dry ice and ethylene glycol (antifreeze) in an insulated container to obtain temperatures below 0°C. Experiment with bacteria of various ages, the rate and temperature at which you freeze the bacteria, the composition of the media in which they are frozen, the length of time they are kept frozen, and the rate and temperature at which you thaw them. You can check their survival by streaking them on nutrient agar and counting the number of colonies that develop.

THE DEBATE ENDS

When first seen with a microscope, bacteria and other microorganisms provided fuel for those who believed in spontaneous generation. The debate became so heated that in 1860 the French Academy of Science offered a prize to the scientist who would finally put this question to rest.

In 1864, Louis Pasteur claimed the prize. Pasteur prepared infusions of sugar and yeast, placed them in flasks, and boiled them for two minutes. He divided the flasks into several groups, each treated differently. He heated the neck of some to form a long curve shaped like a swan's neck.

Pasteur boiled the infusions a second time. As the steam passed out the neck, it killed any microorganisms trapped there. As air entered the neck, any microorganisms would settle on the curved walls and not reach the infusion. All these flasks remained free of microorganisms and have remained so even till today, as you can see by visiting the museum in Paris where they are on display!

You can repeat Pasteur's experiments, perhaps trying different infusion preparations. Vary the length of boiling or sterilize your flasks in a pressure cooker. Try a different shape for the neck of your flasks. Perhaps you can design a completely different experiment to test the idea of spontaneous generation.

If Pasteur's experiments demonstrated that simple life forms such as bacteria did not originate spontaneously, they did not eliminate the possibility that spontaneous generation might have been responsible for the *first* life form on earth.

Scientists have evidence indicating the age of the earth to be more than 4 billion years. The first life form may have appeared over 3 billion years ago. In the 1920s, the Russian scientist A. I. Oparin suggested that under the right conditions the gases of the primitive atmosphere may have collected to form more complex materials, including the first cell. However, Pasteur's experiments rejecting spontaneous generation were so convincing that scientists refused to accept this possibility.

In the 1950s, Stanley Miller and Harold Urey conducted an experiment (see Figure 6) in which they mixed the gases thought to have been present 4 billion years ago under conditions believed to exist at that time. After 24 hours, they discovered that complex chemicals had formed from these simple gases.

Scientists have been able to clump these chemicals into more complex and larger groups known as coarcer-

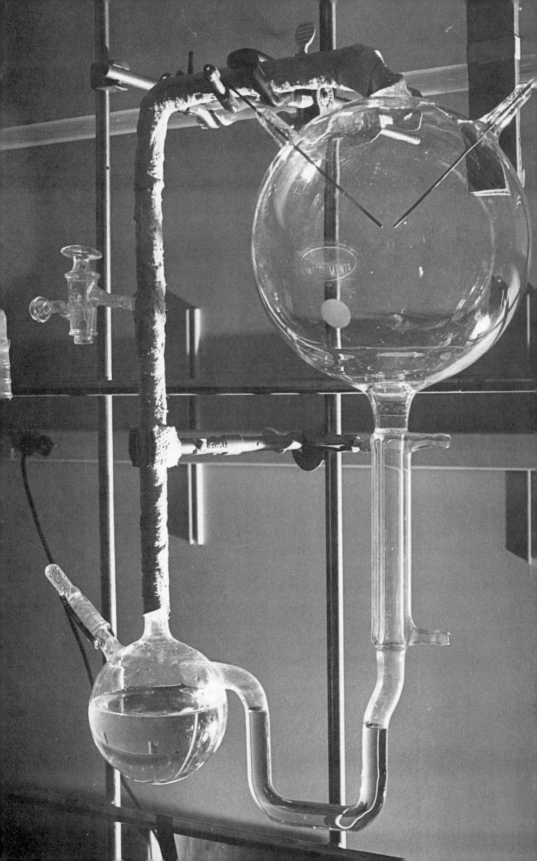

vates. Coarcervates can be formed by mixing together different chemicals under the proper conditions. Dissolve some gelatin and gum arabic in water. Examine a drop of this solution under low-power magnification. Describe what you see.

Slowly add dilute hydrochloric acid drop by drop until the solution turns cloudy. Be careful since hydrochloric acid can burn your skin or irritate your eyes. Examine a drop of the cloudy solution with a microscope and describe any differences you observe.

Compare your coarcervates with an amoeba and describe any similarities. Try other chemicals to make coarcervates. See how temperature changes, differences in the concentration of chemicals used, and ultraviolet light affect these coarcervates.

Chemicals are of interest to biologists not only because of their role in forming coarcervates but also because of their function in all living things. In the next chapter, you will learn how to explore some of the important chemicals of life.

FIGURE 6. UNDER CERTAIN CONDITIONS ESTABLISHED BY SPECIAL APPARATUS, GASES THOUGHT TO BE PART OF THE PRIMITIVE ATMOSPHERE COMBINE TO FORM AMINO ACIDS. SHOWN HERE IS THE EQUIPMENT USED BY STANLEY MILLER IN HIS INVESTIGATIONS INTO THE ORIGIN OF LIFE ON EARTH.

3

CHEMICALS
IN LIVING THINGS

To understand how living things function, you must first know something about the chemicals present in most organisms. Everything an organism does, whether it's digestion, respiration, or any other process, depends on chemicals reacting with one another. Biologists are continually studying these chemicals and how they react. After all, there are so many. One bacterial cell contains over 5,000 different chemicals, while one of your cells has twice that number!

In this chapter, you will be introduced to only some of these chemicals—those that play a major role in biological processes. If you decide to do a project on one of these chemicals, you may make an interesting discovery about its role in living things.

WATER

Wherever there is life, there is water. Water is the most abundant chemical in living things, making up from 50% to 98% of the weight of an organism. This water, which is needed for such biological processes as digestion and circulation, must be obtained from the environment.

Without this water, these biological processes would slow down and eventually stop. The organism would die.

On the other hand, an organism may have too much water at certain times. Excess water might cause the organism to swell, burst, and die. To prevent this from happening, the organism must get rid of the water before any damage is done. Obviously, all organisms must maintain just the right amount of water needed to survive.

The major mechanism used by most organisms for obtaining and eliminating water is diffusion. Diffusion occurs any time a substance such as water moves from a region of higher concentration to one of a lower concentration. Before entering or leaving an organism, however, water must diffuse through the membrane surrounding each cell. This diffusion of water through a membrane is called osmosis. Osmosis results in an equal concentration of water on both sides of the membrane. This can cause some serious problems for aquatic organisms.

Consider one-celled organisms living in fresh water. The water concentration in the environment is higher than that inside the organism. Consequently, water diffuses into the cell. Without any means of eliminating this water, the organism would swell and probably burst. Fortunately, these organisms can get rid of excess water with the help of a special structure called a contractile vacuole (see Figure 7).

The contractile vacuole collects water from various parts of the cell and pumps it out to the environment. Use a microscope to locate the contractile vacuole in an amoeba or paramecium. If you look closely, the contractile vacuole will suddenly pop and disappear. Count how many times it bursts to expel water during a 5-minute period.

Following are ideas for projects.

- Investigate the effects of different salt concentrations on the rate at which the contractile vacuole expels water. See if the effects vary depending on the type of salt used. Try sodium

contractile vacuole

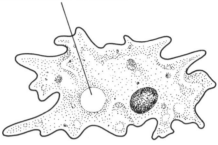

Figure 7. The contractile vacuole in *Amoeba* helps to regulate the water content of the organism. This vacuole fills up with water, then suddenly bursts to expel the water into the environment.

chloride, potassium sulfate, calcium carbonate, and magnesium acetate. Check out the effect of placing the organism in distilled water. Explore other types of environmental changes including variations in temperature, acidity levels, and light intensity.

• The pumping mechanism of a contractile vacuole requires energy. This energy is supplied by the chemical adenosine triphosphate, abbreviated ATP. Certain chemicals, like 2,4-dinitrophenol, can inhibit the amount of ATP produced by an organism. Plan a project to investigate the relationship between an ATP inhibitor and the action of contractile vacuoles. Attempt to identify a substance that accelerates the pumping action of contractile vacuoles. Design an experiment to test whether it speeds up their action by promoting the production of ATP.

- Like their freshwater relatives, one-celled organisms living in saltwater also face a problem. Since their water concentration is higher than that of their environment, these organisms tend to lose water. Many of these organisms are surrounded by brightly colored shells to prevent water loss. Although each shell is microscopic, large numbers accumulate as the organisms die and form massive structures like the white cliffs of Dover in England. Others form large, thick deposits on land and under certain rock formations where oil is often located.

  If you can collect these organisms, undertake a project to photograph these beautiful shells. The shapes and colors depend on what chemicals are present. Include an analysis of each shell type to identify the chemicals present. Refer to the bibliography for references on how to identify elements like silicon, compounds like calcium carbonate, organic substances like proteins, and other chemicals present in these shells.

WATER BALANCE IN LARGER ORGANISMS

Regulating the internal concentration of water is also a problem for larger organisms, especially those living in environments such as estuaries and salt marshes. Here the water and salt concentrations vary over a wide range, depending on tides, currents, rainfall, and land erosion. Animals living in these areas must have the ability to regulate their internal water concentration despite environmental fluctuations.

Select an organism, such as a snail or crab that lives in an estuary or salt marsh (be sure to check local regulations governing the collection of such organisms). Design a project to determine how well it adapts to changes in water concentrations. You can use changes in the organism's weight as a measure of how much water it retains. Compare different organisms to see which one best controls its internal water concentration. Conduct your study at different times of the year to see if the organism can better regulate its water content during a particular season.

Make a comparison between the same type of organism living in different environments: a saltwater crab versus a brackish-water crab or a saltwater snail versus a freshwater snail. Prepare a graph of your results, showing the percent of weight change over a period of time for each water concentration.

If you discover an organism that is a poor regulator of water content, design a project aimed at improving its capability. Experiment with chemical additives. Diuretics are given to people who have trouble eliminating water in their urine. Other drugs cause people to retain water. Check with your doctor or pharmacist for some specific drugs you can test.

PLANTS

Unlike many animals, most plants cannot survive in brackish water or saltwater areas. The roots of these plants lose water by osmosis. Some plants, known as halophytes, can survive under such conditions. The common names of some halophytes growing near the seashore are pickleweed and Palmer's grass (see Figure 8). These plants have mechanisms to get rid of the excess salt. Some expel the salt back into the soil; others store it in special structures where it is washed away by the rain or tides.

Biologists are interested in halophytes not only because of their ability to regulate water content but also because of their potential use as crop plants in areas where fresh water is scarce. Scientists are trying to change such conventional crop plants as corn, wheat, and soybeans to be more like halophytes so that they could grow in saltier soils.

Before scientists can accomplish these tasks, they must first learn more about halophytes. Design an experiment to determine the best conditions for growing a

FIGURE 8. PLANTS GROWING NEAR BRACKISH WATER
HAVE INTERESTING WAYS OF GETTING RID OF EXCESS
SALT TO KEEP THEIR WATER CONTENT IN BALANCE.

halophyte. Test different soil compositions, lighting conditions, and salt concentrations.

Do a study to see if halophyte plant parts, especially
the seeds, can be used as food for small animals like ger-
bils and mice. Analyze the chemicals in these plant parts
to determine their usefulness as food supplements for
humans.

MORE-COMPLEX CHEMICALS

After water, the chemicals found in the greatest amount
in an organism include the *organic* compounds. Organic
compounds contain the element carbon, usually in combination with other elements, particularly hydrogen and
oxygen. Organic compounds you are familiar with are
those found in the foods you eat: sugars, fats, and proteins.

Sugars belong to a group of organic compounds
known as carbohydrates. You can test for the presence
of sugars by adding 1 ml of your test sample to 5 ml of
Benedict's solution. When heated in boiling water for at
least 2 minutes, Benedict's solution will turn color if certain sugars are present. The color will vary from green to
yellow to brick red, depending on the amount of sugar
present.

Sugars are combined to form larger compounds
known as starches. A few drops of Lugol's iodine added
to starch will turn blue-black. Compile a list of substances
tested, indicating whether it contains sugar or starch.
Don't limit yourself to foods. Sugars and starches can be
found in unexpected places. Drug manufacturers add
sugar to children's aspirin to make it sweet tasting and
put starch in adult tablets as a filler.

Sugars are the principal source of energy for most living things. The energy content of any food substance is
measured in calories. One calorie is the amount of energy required to raise 1 g of water 1°C. The rise in the water
temperature is measured with the use of a calorimeter.

Although you can use a metal can to construct a
calorimeter, most food substances are difficult to ignite

so that they burn and heat the surrounding water. Construct your own calorimeter using an insulated container (see Figure 9). Test different foods for their caloric content. Prepare a table showing the relationship between the foods tested and the calories yielded per gram. Explain any differences on the basis of the types of organic compounds present in the foods tested.

Most people obtain their minimum daily energy requirements from the foods they eat. But as many as a billion people suffer from malnutrition, often failing to get even the relatively small number of calories they need to keep alive. Scientists are experimenting with ways to feed the world's growing population.

One promising method involves grinding fish, including the bones and organs, to produce a powder that can be added as a high-energy supplement to various foods. Design a project to prepare a dietary supplement that is nutritious, containing not only the organic food compounds but also vitamins and minerals. Test your supplement on a small animal population to see if it supplies both the materials needed for growth and the energy required for their biological processes.

Here are some more ideas for projects.

- Fats contain more energy than any other food. Compared to sugars or proteins, they can yield almost three times the amount of energy. Fats belong to a group of organic compounds known as lipids. If you tested for sugars and starches, add lipids to your list. One lipid test involves spreading a small amount of the sample on a piece of brown wrapping paper. Upon drying, a grease spot will appear if a lipid is present. Another test is to add a small amount of Sudan IV dye which will dissolve in a lipid.

  Complete your list by testing for proteins. Add 10 drops of Biuret reagent to 5 ml of your sample. A lavender color indicates the presence of protein. Do any of your samples contain sugar, starches, lipids, and proteins?

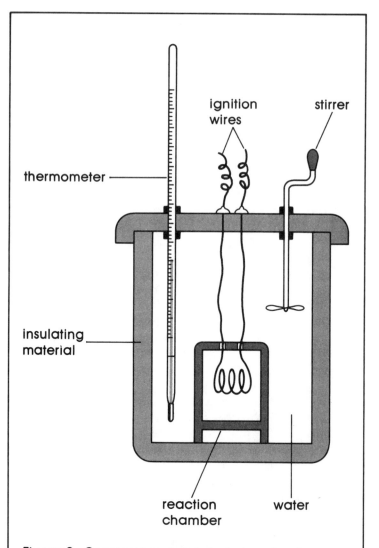

thermometer

ignition
wires

stirrer

insulating
material

reaction
chamber

water

Figure 9. Construct an insulated chamber to
serve as a calorimeter. An electric current ignites
the food sample in the reaction chamber. The
heat from the burning food raises the temperature of the surrounding water.

- Most of the organic compounds in animals are proteins. There are many different types of proteins involved in a variety of biological processes. No matter what its role, every protein is made up of amino acids.

A protein can be broken down into its individual amino acids, which can then be identified using a technique known as chromatography. In the 1950s, scientists used this procedure to determine the amino acid sequence of a protein for the first time. After almost 10 years of work, they knew the structure of insulin.

With modern technology, scientists today can sequence insulin or any other protein about the same size in a few weeks. This information allows them to study evolutionary relationships among organisms by comparing their proteins. They can also analyze abnormal proteins to pinpoint any differences with the normal sequence. One such example is hemoglobin. Normal hemoglobin differs from that found in people with sickle-cell anemia by only one amino acid, out of the 600 present. Yet this minor difference means a much shorter life expectancy for anyone with sickle-cell anemia.

Any project aimed at sequencing the amino acids in a protein would be quite ambitious. However, you might plan a project to identify some common amino acids in a small protein shared by different organisms. You could isolate a protein from the blood sera or egg whites of different animals, or the seeds of different plants. Check the bibliography for references with information on identifying amino acids from isolated proteins.

Rather than obtaining individual amino acids, you can work with intact proteins. After isolating the proteins, you can separate and identify them with a technique known as electrophoresis (see Figure 10). The apparatus used in electrophoresis establishes an electric field. Because of differ-

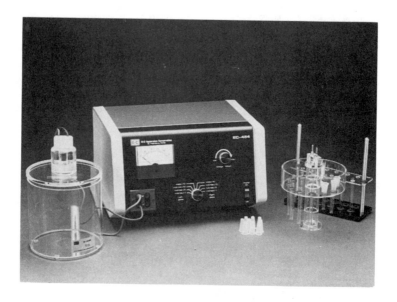

FIGURE 10. THE APPARATUS USED IN ELECTROPHORESIS
SETS UP CHARGED FIELDS TO SEPARATE COMPOUNDS ON
THE BASIS OF THEIR ELECTRICAL PROPERTIES.

ences in the charges they carry, proteins will
behave differently when exposed to this electric
field. The apparatus needed for this type of project is simple and inexpensive. References cited in
the bibliography provide information on electrophoresis.

ENZYMES

One type of protein playing a vital role in all organisms is
the *enzyme*. Enzymes speed up chemical reactions that
are the basis for all biological processes. If these reactions did not occur rapidly, the organism would die.

You can learn a great deal about enzymes by working with just a few chemicals and something you probably love to eat—liver. Liver contains an enzyme called
catalase. This enzyme speeds up the breakdown of

hydrogen peroxide, a poisonous chemical continually produced by organisms.

Pour 5 ml of 3% hydrogen peroxide into a test tube. Be careful since hydrogen peroxide is not only poisonous but can also irritate your skin and eyes. Be sure to wear protective eye goggles.

Add a piece of liver about the size of a rice grain and observe what happens. After the reaction stops, divide the contents into two test tubes. Add another piece of liver to one and 5 ml of fresh hydrogen peroxide to the other. Based on your observations, did the liver, hydrogen peroxide, or both remain unchanged after the first reaction?

Plan a project to test the effects of various factors on enzyme action. Gauge their effectiveness by measuring the height of the gas bubbles produced by the reaction. Vary the temperature. Freeze the liver overnight and then test its effectiveness after thawing. Boil the liver in water for 10 minutes before adding it to the hydrogen peroxide. Check other food products for catalase.

Alter the acidity and alkalinity of the solution by adding different concentrations of an acid or base. Vary the amounts of liver and hydrogen peroxide to see what concentrations work best.

A more precise way of testing the relationship between enzyme concentration and the rate of the reaction can be made by using your saliva. Saliva contains an enzyme capable of breaking down starch.

Chew a piece of gum to stimulate the release of saliva. Collect 5 ml of your saliva in a test tube. Dilute the saliva with distilled water to prepare different concentrations. For example, mix 1 ml of saliva with 9 ml of water to dilute it 10 times. Add 1 ml of this diluted solution to 9 ml of water to make a sample that is 100 times more dilute than the original saliva.

Test the action of the enzyme in saliva on a 0.5% starch solution made up in a 0.25% sodium chloride solution. After mixing the starch with enzyme, check at regular intervals for any remaining starch by adding a few drops of Lugol's iodine. Record the time and continue testing until no color change is noticed. Prepare a graph, plotting the rate of the reaction (by dividing the time into 1) versus the concentration of the saliva.

Rather than using the enzyme in liver or saliva, isolate a different enzyme from either an animal or plant. Since isolating an enzyme can be difficult, you may want to work with extracts from a plant or animal. For example, mix a small plant with some sand and water in a mortar. Grind it with a pestle till you form a paste. Filter the paste through cheesecloth to collect the liquid extract. If this extract shows enzymatic activity, experiment with various ways to influence its action.

Some enzymes require other chemicals in order to function. These chemicals are called coenzymes. Some salts and vitamins have been shown to work as coenzymes. Plan a project to see if your enzyme works better if another chemical is present. On the other hand, enzyme action can be inhibited by certain chemicals. For example, penicillin inhibits the action of a bacterial enzyme. Design an experiment to identify an inhibitor for your enzyme.

If you tested the effects of temperature changes, you probably discovered an optimum range for enzyme action. However, not all enzymes function best in this range. For example, the characteristic color of Siamese cats depends on enzymes that become active only at low temperatures. This enzyme controls the production of the dark pigment in the face, ears, and paws.

Plan a project to see what other animals have enzymes affected by temperature changes. Work with a small animal normally found in either a very warm or cold climate. Look for any changes in physical appearance as you alter the temperature. If any change occurs, prove that it is the result of enzyme action. By the way, if you plan to enter your project in a science fair, check on regulations regarding the use of animals. Many science fairs either prohibit experiments with vertebrates or have strict guidelines on their use.

If working with small animals is a problem, you can conduct a number of projects with enzymes by using microorganisms. Lysozyme is an enzyme found in tears, saliva, milk, and many other fluids of different animals. This enzyme breaks down the wall surrounding bacterial cells. Try to detect lysozyme by adding small drops of various fluids to bacteria growing on agar cultures. If lysozyme is present, the bacteria will be destroyed and replaced by a clear area on the plate. You can extend this project by analyzing the various lysozymes to see what amino acids they have in common.

Bacteria in turn use enzymes to break down certain substances. One enzyme they secrete is gelatinase to cut proteins into smaller pieces so that they can be absorbed by the bacteria. You can study the action of this enzyme by using an inoculating needle to insert different bacteria into test tubes containing sterile gelatin. Look for any melting of the solid gelatin.

Obviously, only a small fraction of the several thousand different chemicals found in living things can be covered in one chapter. Even those you have read about have a much longer story to tell. Some of them play a role in the two biological processes covered in the next chapter: photosynthesis and respiration.

4

PHOTOSYNTHESIS AND RESPIRATION

Plants take two simple chemicals, carbon dioxide and water, and use light energy to change them into sugar and oxygen. This is photosynthesis. In turn, both plants and animals use the oxygen to break down these sugars, along with other chemicals, to obtain the energy they require. As a result of this process, they release carbon dioxide and water. This is respiration.

As you can see, photosynthesis and respiration depend on each other. The chemicals produced by one are used by the other, resulting in a biological balance. You can observe this balance by setting up an aquarium with both plants and animals. Try to establish the proper conditions so that you won't have to add any food or supply additional oxygen.

Organisms known as algae can serve as a food source. If you have a tropical fish aquarium, you may have seen algae growing as a green or red film on the glass. Strong sunlight promotes algae growth. Include animals like snails that eat algae and require less oxygen than fish. Vary the amount of light and water temperature to obtain just the right balance between the plants and animals. After a few weeks, your project may not look too attractive, but it will demonstrate the relationship between photosynthesis and respiration.

A COLORFUL PROCESS

Plants must absorb light energy before they can use it for photosynthesis. Pigments are the chemicals responsible for absorbing light. Different plants use various pigments in photosynthesis, but the most common one is chlorophyll, which gives the plant its green color. Because of its abundance, chlorophyll masks the other pigments used in photosynthesis: the reds, yellows, and oranges.

To remove the pigments from a plant, boil some chopped-up leaves in ethanol until you have a concentrated extract with a dark green color. Since ethanol is flammable, be careful while working with the hot plate or Bunsen burner.

Use paper chromatography to separate the pigments (see Figure 11). Apply the pigment extract with a toothpick in a very thin line, allowing each one to dry before the next application. The finer and darker the line, the better the separation. Use a mixture of 95 parts petroleum ether to 5 parts acetone as the solvent. Remove the strip when the solvent has risen to a point near the top of the paper. The different pigments will be visible as the paper dries.

Check different types of leaves for their pigments. Calculate the R_f value for each pigment. The R_f value represents a ratio between the distances traveled by the pigment and solvent. To calculate an R_f value, divide the distance traveled by the pigment by that traveled by the solvent (see Figure 12). See how the amount of each pigment varies according to the season. Vary the proportion of petroleum ether to acetone to see which gives the best separation.

Each pigment absorbs light of a different wavelength. Chlorophyll absorbs all colors except green; because it reflects green, chlorophyll appears green. The absorption pattern of a pigment is known as its absorption spectrum.

FIGURE 11. USE PAPER CHROMATOGRAPHY TO
SEPARATE THE PIGMENTS EXTRACTED FROM PLANTS.
APPLY THE PIGMENT IN A THIN LINE. THE FINER AND
DARKER THE LINE, THE BETTER THE SEPARATION.

If a spectrophotometer is available, you can analyze chlorophyll and other pigments for their absorption spectra. Change the wavelength on the spectrophotometer from 400 to 650 nanometers in 25-nanometer increments. Measure how much light is absorbed by the pigment for each wavelength. Compare different plants to see if their pigments absorb light of the same wavelengths. Graph your results, plotting the absorbance on the vertical scale and the wavelength on the horizontal scale. Draw as many conclusions as possible about light, pigments, and photosynthesis from your results.

You may have discovered that certain wavelengths are strongly absorbed by plant pigments. This suggests that these wavelengths are the ones used in photosynthesis. However, direct experimental proof is lacking. One way to obtain such evidence is to discover a con-

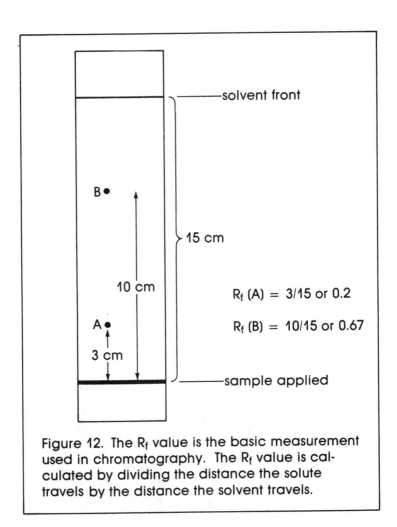

Figure 12. The R_f value is the basic measurement used in chromatography. The R_f value is calculated by dividing the distance the solute travels by the distance the solvent travels.

nection between a particular wavelength and a product of photosynthesis, either oxygen or sugar.

Plants combine sugars to make starches. If you first boil a leaf in alcohol to remove the pigments, you can then test for starch by covering the leaf with a small amount of Lugol's iodine. The darker the blue-black color, the more starch present. However, it is difficult to distinguish between different intensities of a blue-black color.

A more precise way to determine the most effective wavelength involves measuring the amount of oxygen gas released by a plant. The simplest way is to count the number of oxygen bubbles given off by the plant in one minute. Place a freshwater plant such as *Elodea* in a test tube filled with a 3% sodium bicarbonate solution. Expose the plant to different wavelengths of light. You can use colored filters placed between a white light and the test tube to obtain different wavelengths, for example, a red one for red light.

To be even more precise, use a manometer (see Figure 13). Although their design may differ, all manometers operate on the same principle: As the volume of a gas changes, a fluid moves in a U-shaped tube. A syringe is used to return the fluid to its original level. The original and final positions of the syringe plunger are recorded. The difference represents the volume of gas that caused the fluid to move.

FIGURE 13. AS THE VOLUME OF A GAS CHANGES, THE FLUID IN THE U-SHAPED TUBE OF A MANOMETER MOVES. A SYRINGE IS USED TO RETURN THE FLUID TO ITS ORIGINAL LEVEL.

Numerous quantitative projects are possible with a simple manometer. Not only can you test different wavelengths, but you can also try various light intensities and temperatures. Determine the light intensity and temperature beyond which no further increase in the rate of photosynthesis is possible.

Vary the amount of carbon dioxide available to the plant by using different sodium bicarbonate concentrations. The bicarbonate serves as the carbon dioxide source. See if adding other salts affects the photosynthetic rate. You can carry out a project to see if different aquatic plants react the same way. Design a method to measure the volume of oxygen gas produced by land plants.

The oxygen released in photosynthesis comes from the splitting of water by light energy. You can duplicate this process by passing an electric current through water; hydrogen and oxygen gases will be produced in a 2:1 ratio. Many details about how plants produce oxygen from water remain unanswered. Scientists believe that electrons are removed from water and eventually wind up with chlorophyll, but they don't know all the steps. Perhaps you can carry out a project to add some information on this process.

THE DARK SIDE OF PHOTOSYNTHESIS

Plants do not use light energy directly to change carbon dioxide into sugar. This process occurs in what is known as the dark reaction of photosynthesis. The dark reaction does, however, depend on products made by the plant's use of light energy. Consequently, there are two stages to photosynthesis: a light reaction and a dark reaction.

Unfortunately, adequate amounts of carbon dioxide are not always available for plants to carry out the dark reaction. When this occurs, the rate of photosynthesis drops. Some plants are better able to deal with lower carbon dioxide concentrations. Known as C4 plants, they can thrive in high light intensities, hot temperatures, and dry conditions. On the other hand, those known as C3 plants photosynthesize better with less light, moderate temperatures, and humid days.

Over 100 species of C4 plants have been identified, including sugarcane, crabgrass, and corn. Compared to the efficiency of C3 plants under certain conditions, their efficiency of photosynthesis is phenomenal: The plants grow faster and produce larger crops for farmers. Scientists are trying to alter some C3 crop plants to produce food more quickly and efficiently. You could make a significant contribution to research on improving or increasing the world's food supply by carrying out a project in this area.

RESPIRATION WITHOUT OXYGEN

Energy is needed to carry out all biological processes, from digestion in humans to the action of contractile vacuoles in amoeba. This energy, as you may recall from the discussion of contractile vacuoles in Chapter 2, is supplied by ATP. In most organisms, the chemical energy in foods is stored in ATP through two processes: glycolysis and respiration.

Glycolysis converts the sugar glucose into another chemical called pyruvic acid. This process can operate without oxygen. In the absence of oxygen, pyruvic acid is then changed into either ethanol or lactic acid, depending on the organism. For example, yeast contain enzymes capable of turning fruit juices into alcohol in a process called fermentation.

Fermentation by yeast (see Figure 14) is also important to bakers. But bakers are more interested in the carbon dioxide, which causes the dough to rise. To study fermentation, make bread using yeast. Compare it to bread made with baking soda or baking powder, two chemicals often used in place of yeast. Test different oven temperatures to see which yields the "fluffiest" bread. By the way, don't worry about any alcohol since it evaporates in the oven.

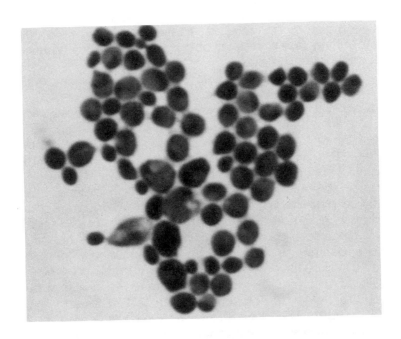

FIGURE 14. YEAST CELLS RESPIRE, PRODUCING
ALCOHOL AND CARBON DIOXIDE. THIS PROCESS,
CALLED FERMENTATION, OCCURS WITHOUT OXYGEN.
(ORIGINAL MAGNIFICATION: 1,000 TIMES.)

Other organisms, including humans, change glucose in the absence of oxygen into a different chemical known as lactic acid. Whenever you exercise strenuously, lactic acid collects in your muscles, causing soreness and fatigue. In some cases, so much lactic acid accumulates that the muscles can't function at all. Many marathon runners reach this point near the end of the race. They simply collapse in extreme pain, while others go on to the finish.

Scientists are trying to discover the biological basis of why some runners can complete a marathon without serious muscle problems. Studies show that runners switch to fats for energy after using all their stored glucose. This switch causes an increase in the acidity of the blood, producing severe distress and preventing many runners from finishing the race.

Some research work indicates that women can switch to using fats more easily than men. If you are interested in sports, design a project to explain why women are better able to do this. You can also develop a project aimed at increasing an athlete's capacity to compete. One way to accomplish this goal is to regulate the amount of carbohydrates in the diet. One week before a race, some marathon runners jog long distances followed by 3 days of a low-carbohydrate diet and then 3 days of high-carbohydrate intake.

Since science fairs usually prohibit the use of humans as experimental subjects, work with a small animal such as a mouse or hamster. Both these animals are vertebrates, so check for guidelines on their use in a science project. Write to Science Service, 1719 N Street N.W., Washington, DC 20036 for information on projects involving vertebrates. Design a way of having the animal perform some sustained activity. Manipulate the animal's diet and record changes in the amount of time the animal can carry out this activity. You can measure the amount of oxygen used by the animal with the help of a respirometer (see Figure 15).

As the animal uses oxygen, the air pressure in the jar of the respirometer will fall. The higher pressure outside will force the colored liquid in the tube toward the container. By measuring the distance traveled by the liquid in a given time, you can determine the animal's rate of oxygen uptake.

RESPIRATION WITH OXYGEN

In the presence of oxygen, pyruvic acid is broken down more completely and releases a greater amount of energy than glycolysis. The complete oxidation of glucose produces water and carbon dioxide.

There's a simple way to get an approximate measurement of the amount of carbon dioxide produced in

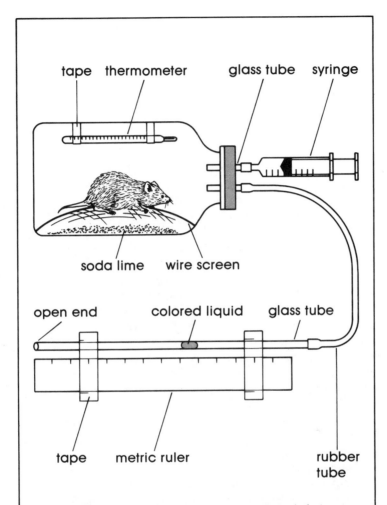

tape   thermometer   glass tube   syringe

soda lime   wire screen

open end   colored liquid   glass tube

tape   metric ruler   rubber tube

Figure 15. Use some inexpensive materials to construct a respirometer which can measure the oxygen consumption of a mouse or other small animal. The soda lime absorbs the carbon dioxide gas given off by the animal. Insert the colored liquid into the glass tube at the open end.

respiration. Add 100 ml of tap water to a flask. Breathe into the water through a straw for 1 minute. Add 5 drops of phenolpthalein. Record how much 0.4% sodium hydroxide solution you must add to turn this solution a light pink color. After subtracting the amount needed to turn just tap water pink, multiply the milliliters of sodium hydroxide added to your test solution by 10. This product equals the amount of carbon dioxide, expressed in a unit called micromoles.

Record the amount of carbon dioxide produced after performing different activities: sleeping, sitting, mild and vigorous exercise, or taking a test. Sample classmates to see how much variation exists. Compare athletes with the rest of the class. Check your results from different weight groups and ages. See if one sex on the average produces more carbon dioxide.

Plants also produce carbon dioxide as a result of respiration. You can study plant respiration by measuring the amount of oxygen taken up by seeds with the help of a manometer. Wrap a small amount of ascarite in cheesecloth. Ascarite, which can be purchased from a scientific supply company, is a chemical that absorbs gases. Place the ascarite in the tube, cover it with a loose wad of cheesecloth, and then add some germinating bean or pea seeds. Since the ascarite absorbs carbon dioxide and water vapor, any volume change is caused by oxygen uptake. If the change is too rapid or slow, remove or add seeds as needed.

Measure oxygen use as a function of temperature changes. Compare different seeds for their rate of respiration. Identify other factors capable of affecting the respiration rate of germinating seeds. Such a factor might be useful in promoting a more rapid growth rate.

Another way to observe respiration in plants involves trapping the carbon dioxide. See what happens to a bromothymol blue solution as you add carbon dioxide by blowing into it with a straw. With this information, design an experiment to test the rate of respiration in the leaves of different plants. Investigate whether plants placed in the light for 24 hours respire at the same rate as those kept in the dark for the same amount of time. Check if the rate of respiration varies according to the season.

THE ROLE OF OXYGEN

Most students mistakenly believe that the oxygen they breathe in turns into the carbon dioxide they breathe out. In fact, the oxygen used in respiration becomes part of water. One problem that has confronted biologists for many years is how this process works. A project in this area may shed some light on the details of how cells can combine various subtances with oxygen to make water. Other unanswered questions about how cells function are discussed in the next chapter.

5

CELL STRUCTURE
AND FUNCTION

If you have ever explored the microscopic world of a single drop of pond water, you were probably impressed by the many different kinds of microorganisms you discovered. But without a powerful microscope to peer into these tiny creatures, you may not have been able to pick out much detail. Here's a chance to examine the structure of more complex cells—those making up both plants and animals.

Remove a thin layer from an onion. Select a single, healthy leaf from an *Elodea* plant. Slice a paper-thin section of a potato. Gently scrape the lining of your mouth with the flat edge of a toothpick. Obtain some eggs from a sea urchin. Remove the wings from a fly.

Prepare a wet mount of each specimen. Using both low-and high-power objective lenses, sketch what you see. Add a drop of either methylene blue or Lugol's iodine stain to each specimen. Note any differences in appearance after adding the stain.

Extend your project by comparing an unstained specimen using different types of microscopes. Use a phase-contrast, differential-interference, or dark-field microscope. These microscopes reveal features difficult to

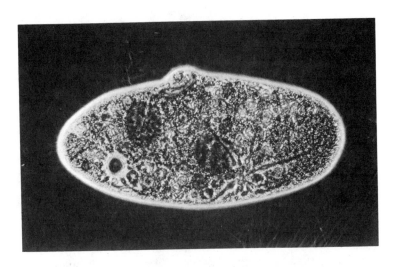

FIGURE 16. A PHASE-CONTRAST MICROSCOPE
REVEALS THE DETAILS OF THE INTERNAL STRUCTURE
OF SUCH SMALL ORGANISMS AS *PARAMECIUM.*

detect with an ordinary light microscope (see Figure 16). If you are interested in photography, mount a camera to the body tube of the microscope to take pictures of your specimens. You can also attach a video camera to a microscope to tape the action of live cells. A careful analysis of the videotape might reveal some interesting aspect of a cell's structure or function.

No matter what type of microscope you use, you'll undoubtedly be impressed by the variety of cells. Cells come in many different shapes and sizes. They vary in shape from the rectangular *Elodea* cell to the round sea urchin egg. They vary in size from your small cheek cell to a large chicken egg. Yet all cells share many common features.

For example, all cells are surrounded by a membrane. This membrane controls what enters and leaves the cell. As you may recall from Chapter 2, one such substance is water. Because cell membranes allow only certain substances to pass through them, they are said to be semipermeable. You can study what controls the movement of materials across the cell membrane with the use of dialysis tubing. This tubing is used in dialysis machines to filter out waste products from the blood of people with kidney disease.

Dissolve some sugar, starch, salt, and gelatin or egg white (protein) in distilled water. Pour the solution into a piece of dialysis tubing. Insert a 10-ml pipette into one end of the tubing and place it in a beaker of distilled water (see Figure 17). After 30 minutes, record the height of the water in the pipette. Test the contents of the beaker and dialysis tubing for sugar, starch, salt, and protein. If the solution turns cloudy when a few drops of 5% silver nitrate are added, salt is present. Based on your results, determine which substances crossed the membrane. Explain why only certain substances crossed the membrane. Explain why only certain substances can diffuse through the membrane. Investigate the effects of increasing the temperature or pressure on the diffusion of these substances.

Experiment with other chemicals to test whether they can pass through the membrane. Explore ways of changing a substance that cannot diffuse so that it will pass through the membrane. Try heating or exposing the chemical to enzyme action. Test the effects of boiling water, exposure to mild acids or bases, and stretching to see if you can alter the permeability of the dialysis tubing.

As you may remember from Chapter 2, diffusion and osmosis result in equal concentrations on both sides of a membrane. In many cases, however, cells must obtain as many nutrients as possible while eliminating as much waste as possible. This imbalance cannot occur by diffusion or osmosis. To accomplish this, cells use a process called active transport. This process moves substances from a lower concentration to a higher one, in effect going against what would naturally happen. Active transport is especially important in freshwater animals.

Frogs, for example, lose salt through their skin and urine to the environment. Their skin cells are able to carry

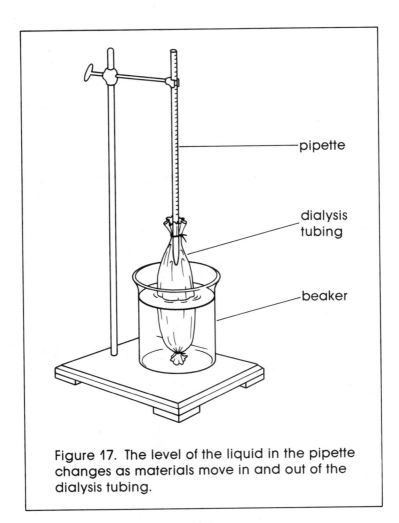

Figure 17. The level of the liquid in the pipette changes as materials move in and out of the dialysis tubing.

out active transport to retrieve this lost salt, maintaining a constant internal concentration. You can conduct a project on active transport with a natural membrane by stripping the skin from a frog's leg and tying off both ends after filling it with Ringer's solution.

You can purchase Ringer's solution (which has the same salt content as the frog's cells) or you can make it.

Dissolve 0.14 g of potassium chloride, 6.50 g of sodium chloride, 0.12 g of calcium chloride, and 0.20 g of sodium bicarbonate in enough distilled water to make 1 liter of solution. If kept moist with Ringer's solution, the skin can be used for several hours after removal from the frog.

Suspend the membrane sacs in a beaker. Use a small air pump to supply oxygen. Vary the types and concentrations of salt solutions used to bathe the sacs. Be sure to use both sodium and potassium salts since they are known to play a role in active transport. Expose the sacs for various lengths of time. Find the optimum conditions for maintaining a constant internal salt concentration. Do a comparative study on different species of frogs.

You will need some knowledge of electricity and special equipment to measure the movement of salts across the membrane. Consult a physics teacher for help and advice.

Like frogs, most plants face the problem of losing salt and gaining water. Plant cells, especially those in the roots, must use active transport to obtain the salts needed for growth. You can use *Elodea* to study active transport in plant cells. In light, the under surface of their leaves actively uptakes calcium from the water, while the upper surface secretes any excess back into the environment.

Prepare a saturated solution of calcium carbonate by dissolving as much of the salt as possible in tap water that has been allowed to sit for a few days. Add a small amount of phenolpthalein. If the solution is pink, blow into it through a straw until it becomes colorless.

Submerge a plant in this solution. If calcium salts are actively secreted by the cells on the upper surface of the leaf, the solution surrounding this area will become alkaline and turn pink because of the phenolpthalein. Add different salts to study their effect on active transport. Vary the salt concentrations, including that of calcium carbonate, to determine the point at which inhibition of active transport occurs. Can you identify a salt that is the most effective inhibitor? Check if different light intensities and wavelengths affect active transport in plants.

Regardless of whether the cell membranes are found in plants or animals, biologists do not know how they carry out active transport. Several models have been suggested involving special proteins called carriers. These carriers pick up a substance on one side on the' membrane and dump it on the other. Exactly how they accomplish this task is not clear, although scientists know active transport requires large amounts of energy. They estimate that more than a third of the ATP used by a resting animal goes for active transport. Perhaps you can spend some of the remaining energy on a project to identify a carrier protein or explain how one operates.

PLANTS PUT UP
A WALL

Plant cells, unlike those of animals, have a cell wall surrounding the cell membrane. This cell wall is rigid. As water moves into a plant cell, it pushes the membrane against the cell wall creating an internal pressure known as turgor. Turgor keeps the cell walls stiff and the plant crisp. If water leaves the cell, the cell membrane shrinks and the plant wilts.

Use *Elodea* to study turgor. Examine cells exposed to various salts, lighting conditions, and carbon dioxide concentrations with a microscope to observe the cell membrane. When turgor is reduced, the cell membrane will pull away from the cell wall (see Figure 18). Manipulate environmental conditions to restore turgor. You can also investigate turgor in guard cells, which control the opening and closing of the pores in leaves during photosynthesis.

WHAT'S INSIDE
THE MEMBRANE?

With the help of the electron microscope, biologists have been able to probe into the cell's interior to study the details of its structure. The electron microscope can magnify objects as much as 1,000,000 times. Biologists

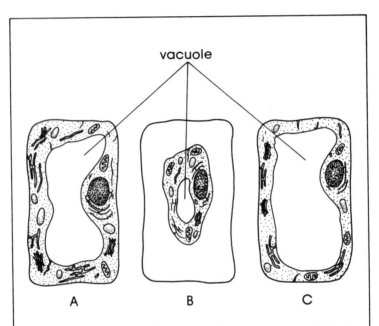

vacuole

A   B   C

Figure 18. Plant cells have both a cell membrane and a cell wall. Under normal conditions (A), a large vacuole containing water fills the cytoplasm, pushing the cell membrane up against the cell wall. As water leaves the cell (B), the cell membrane becomes visible as it shrinks away from the cell wall. As water re-enters the cell (C), the vacuole swells, pushing the membrane back against the cell wall.

usually magnify between 10,000 and 100,000 times to study the cell's interior. A new type of microscope, called the scanning electron microscope, allows scientists to obtain high magnification studies of living specimens. The scanning electron microscope also provides a good image of the three-dimensional structure of objects (see Figure 19).

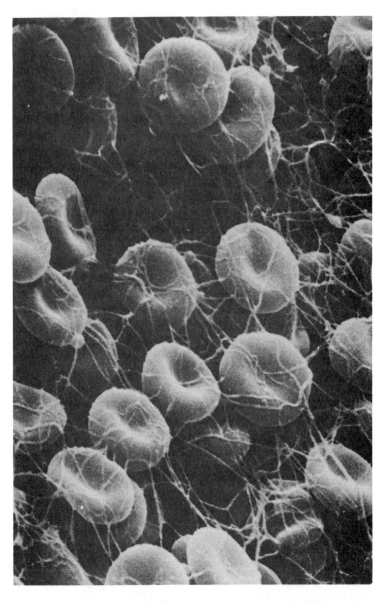

FIGURE 19. THE THREE-DIMENSIONAL STRUCTURE OF
OBJECTS, SUCH AS THESE HUMAN RED BLOOD CELLS, CAN BE
STUDIED WITH A SCANNING ELECTRON MICROSCOPE.

If you are interested in a project involving the use of an electron microscope, contact a local university or research lab. You could conduct a project to study the detailed structure of one of the cell's components. In exchange for the use of their equipment, you could volunteer your services in helping them prepare their specimens for viewing under the electron microscope.

Another technique that has provided information about the cell's interior is autoradiography. Radioactive chemicals known as tracers are added to cells growing in tissue culture. The cells are removed and placed on microscope slides coated with a photosensitive film. Radiation strikes this coating, producing black spots when the film is developed.

Radioactive tracers can be used to study how certain materials are processed by cells. After verifying that the tracer can be taken up by the cells, a scientist removes the cells at set intervals for study. In this way, the path the tracer takes through the cell can be followed.

Working with a low-level radioactive source like tritium (a radioactive form of hydrogen), you could follow the fate of several different chemicals as they are used by cells. For example, if the hydrogen in water were radioactive, you could follow its pathway in photosynthesis. **If your project involves tracers, be sure to work under the supervision of a scientist or professional trained to handle radioactive materials.**

Tracers have been helpful in studying how materials move through the cell, especially between the fluid-filled portion known as the cytoplasm and the central structure called the nucleus. The nucleus is the control center of the cell and is easily visible in most plant and animal cells. A membrane separates the nucleus from the cytoplasm, but pores allow certain substances to move back and forth. A project using radioactive tracers would reveal which substances are exchanged between the nucleus and cytoplasm. You could then investigate ways to affect this exchange: changing the temperature, adding various chemicals, or manipulating the cell's environment in some other way.

CELL DIVISION

The nucleus undergoes a series of changes before a cell can divide in a process called mitosis. Examine a prepared slide of an onion root tip. Observe the various stages through which the cell passes. The dark-stained structures visible in the center are the chromosomes containing the genetic information (see Figure 20). Whenever a cell divides, each of the two cells formed must receive all the parts it needs to function, including a full set of chromosomes.

Investigate cell division by rooting an onion or garlic in water. After the roots sprout, select one that is at least 3 cm long. Place the tip on a clean slide and cut off a section 1 cm from the bottom. Cover this portion with a few drops of 1N hydrochloric acid. Be careful not to spill any acid on your hands. After putting on your protective eye goggles, pass the slide over a low flame from a Bunsen burner two or three times. Blot off any remaining acid. Cover the tip with a few drops of toluidine blue O or aceto-orcein stain. Again pass the slide through the flame and blot dry. Add a drop of fresh stain, apply a cover slip, and place the slide between a paper towel. Press *gently* with your thumb using a steady, firm pressure to crush the onion root tip. Examine the slide with a microscope.

Prepare your slides at different times of the day to see if there is a peak period for mitosis by comparing the number of cells undergoing cell division. Expose the plant to different light and temperature cycles. A project determining the optimum conditions for mitosis would have practical application for growing the plant.

Experiment with ways of affecting cell division by adding various substances to the water used for rooting. Look for any obvious abnormalities: broken or damaged chromosomes, changes in their number, or irregular arrangements. Test the effects of such plant products as nicotine, caffeine, and quinine. Experiment with colchicine, a chemical that allows the chromosomes to double but prevents the cell from dividing. As a consequence,

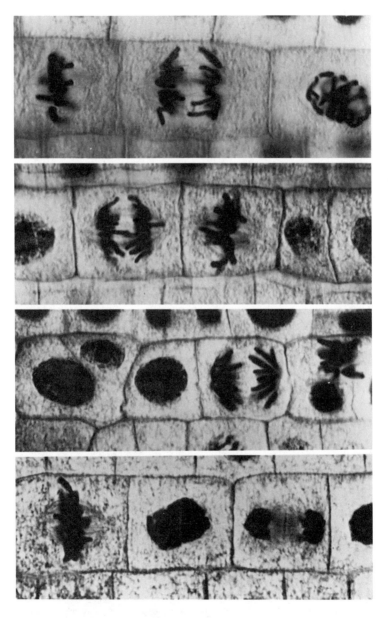

FIGURE 20. CHROMOSOMES ARE CLEARLY VISIBLE IN
THE DIVIDING CELLS FOUND IN AN ONION ROOT TIP.

the cell has an extra set of chromosomes. Biologists have used colchicine to produce plants with larger flowers and bigger fruits. Explore if any of these changes are reversible—can you restore the chromosomes to their original condition?

Normally, cells continue to divide until they touch one another. You can see this process by culturing cells in glass containers containing a culture medium. Several different culture media are available from scientific supply companies. These media contain salts, minerals, nutrients, and antibiotics to prevent contamination by microorganisms.

Cells grown in cultures can be used for a variety of projects. If you can get certain cells to grow in culture, that in itself can be a significant project. Try culturing cells from insects, worms, clams, or starfish. Other projects might involve exploring the effects of adding enzymes, varying the light intensity, or changing the temperature of the culture medium. You could also vary the ingredients used in the culture media to see which combination provides the best environment for cell division.

This is exactly what several scientists did in the early 1960s. They took small pieces of carrots and placed them in Erlenmeyer flasks containing a culture medium that included coconut milk. The flasks were sealed to prevent contamination and gently shaken. The carrot cells grew rapidly. Next, the scientists took individual carrot cells to grow in culture. The cells divided rapidly to form large fragments, which developed into small plants when transferred to agar containing coconut milk. These were the first cloning experiments, producing a complete organism from a single cell.

Carry out a project by cloning carrots, lettuce, or a fern plant. Begin by washing pieces cut from the plant in warm, soapy water. Rinse with sterile distilled water before placing the fragments in a 15% chlorine bleach solution. Shake the container for about 5 minutes. Rinse again with sterile distilled water. Place the plant section in a sterile petri dish containing nutrients and the plant hormone auxin. Expose the dishes to light 12 hours a day for 2 to 3 weeks. A solid mass of unspecialized cells called a *callus* will develop. Use sterilized forceps to remove a small piece of the callus and place it in a test tube of gelatin containing nutrients and two plant hormones, auxin and cytokinin. This growth medium will cause the callus to grow into a fully developed plant.

The right combination of auxin and cytokinin is critical for cloning plant cells. In addition, calcium salts have been shown to modify the action of the hormone mixture. Your project can include an identification of factors affecting the development of a plant clone. Try cloning flowering plants or special strains that have been developed for their high nutritional value or resistance to disease.

Cloning experiments are often unsuccessful because of the constant need for sterile conditions and the maintenance of proper hormone combinations. You may find it worthwhile to begin a cloning project by using a kit purchased from a scientific supply company. Once you've mastered the technique, you can develop some improvement in the method or try it with other plants.

Clones are genetically identical since they are all developed from a single source. Biologists often try to introduce new genetic material into a cell before cloning it. Their object is to produce a new strain more desirable than the original. Perhaps the new strain can better tolerate harsh environments, resist many types of diseases, or grow more rapidly. If a project in this area interests you, you must first explore some basic principles of genetics. This is the subject of the next chapter.

6

GENETICS

While shopping in a supermarket in the summer, you may have noticed small flies gathered near the fresh fruit. These flies have the scientific name *Drosophila melanogaster* and, for obvious reasons, are commonly known as fruit flies. Our understanding of genetics owes much to these fruit flies as a result of their extensive use in laboratory experiments on heredity. There are several reasons why fruit flies are often used in genetic research: They are easy to breed and maintain. Large numbers can be kept in a small bottle with just a little food. Each female fly lays hundreds of eggs at a time, providing a new generation every two weeks.

You can undertake a number of different projects in genetics with the help of fruit flies. All you need are a stereoscopic microscope, ether, an etherizer, vials containing food, a tapered brush, and some flies (see Figure 21). You can purchase the ether and etherizer from a scientific supply company. **Always have good ventilation when working with ether and keep it away from heat since it is extremely flammable. The ether might also put you to sleep!**

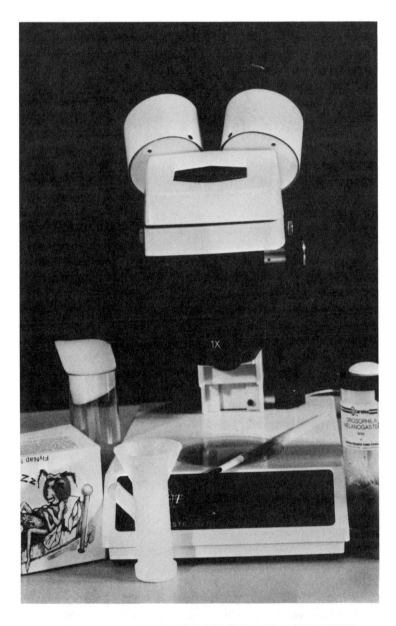

FIGURE 21. A STEREOMICROSCOPE AND A FEW OTHER
ITEMS ARE ALL YOU NEED TO CONDUCT A PROJECT
INVESTIGATING PATTERNS OF HEREDITY IN FRUIT FLIES.

You can buy ready-to-use vials and flies from a scientific supply company. If you want to save money, use baby food jars in place of vials and make your own medium. Cook up a mixture of cornmeal, agar, molasses, water, and a mold preservative. Pour the hot mixture to fill up about a quarter of the vial or jar. The liquid will solidify as the agar hardens. Some yeast sprinkled on the surface will serve as a food source. If the medium is too soft, the flies will get trapped in the food and die.

Once you understand how genetics operates in a fruit fly, you can extend your project to a different organism, either an animal or plant. After all, the father of genetics, Gegor Mendel, worked with pea plants. But you should realize that his work took many years, requiring thousands of plants and a very large garden. Whatever organism you study, check out its suitability for genetic analysis. Be sure you have everything you need, including the time.

FRUIT FLIES

Working with fruit flies is easy and requires little space. Place several drops of ether in the etherizer. Gently tap the vial of flies to knock them to the bottom. Quickly remove the cotton plug from the vial and place it firmly over the etherizer. Tap the vial to transfer all the flies into the etherizer. The ether will start to take effect in a few seconds.

Do not leave the flies in the etherizer for more than a minute. If you do, they will die from overexposure. You can tell a dead fly by its wings sticking straight up from the body. Discard any dead flies in a small jar of oil, commonly known as the morgue.

Remove the bottom from the etherizer and pour the flies onto a white card for microscopic examination. Move the flies around with the brush. Be careful since they injure easily. Females are easy to distinguish from males; they have a larger body that ends in a point. In addition, the rear portion of the male's body is black, whereas the female has alternating dark and light bands extending to the end of her body (see Figure 22).

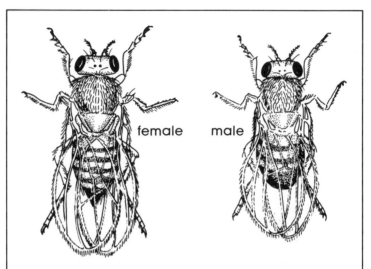

Figure 22. A female *Drosophila*, with her larger body ending in a point, is easy to distinguish from a male.

The flies will start to wake up in about 5 minutes. You can reetherize them by covering the flies with a cotton wad taped to a petri dish cover. Just place a few drops of ether on the cotton before covering the flies. Be careful since flies are more easily killed by a second exposure to ether. When you have finished your examination, place the flies back in a vial and plug with cotton. Set the vial on its side until all the flies have recovered from the ether. In this way, they will not become trapped and die in the food at the bottom.

DETERMINING DOMINANCE

Now that you know how to work with fruit flies, start planning a project. You can begin by identifying a *dominant trait.* Whenever an organism with one trait is mated with an organism having a different trait, only one of the two traits might appear in their offspring. The one that appears is said to be the dominant trait, while the one that did not show up is said to be the recessive trait. The recessive trait will reappear in some offspring of the next generation.

Mate or cross flies with different wing lengths or eye color to determine which trait is dominant. You must use virgin females for all your crosses. In this way, you will know every female is carrying unfertilized eggs since she has not mated with any males. When you introduce the males, you can then be sure that only the traits you wish to study are involved in the cross. To obtain virgin females, remove all the adult flies from a vial. New adults will emerge in about 10 hours. These adult females have not mated and all can be used for your crosses.

Place five virgin female flies with long wings in a vial with five males having short or dumpy wings. Always perform the reciprocal cross: Place five virgin female flies with short wings and five male flies with long wings in another vial. Label all your vials with the date and nature of the cross.

If you store your vials at 25°C, within a week you should see the next generation hatching from the eggs. At this point remove the parents so that you don't confuse them with their offspring, which will appear as adult flies on approximately the 10th day. Etherize them for observation. Continue your observations on the flies that emerge through the 17th day. The more flies included in your results, the better your chances of making an accurate conclusion. Never return flies to their original vials. If you have finished with the first-generation flies, discard them in the morgue.

If you plan to extend your observations to future generations, repeat this procedure: Place virgin females and males from the first generation in a new vial to obtain the second generation which will begin to appear in about another 10 days. Don't forget to include the reciprocal cross whenever you mate flies. You can keep the generations going for as long as you wish.

Check a catalog from a scientific supply company to

see what different types of flies are available to study dominance. Another possibility for your project would be to determine a trait that shows incomplete dominance. For example, incomplete dominance occurs when a red snapdragon is crossed with a white one. All the plants in the next generation have pink flowers. When these pink plants are crossed, red, white, and pink flowers appear in the second generation. Investigate whether a trait in fruit flies behaves in a similar fashion.

Your project can follow the inheritance of two or more traits at the same time. Mate flies with normal wings and red eyes with ones lacking wings and having sepia-colored eyes. Such a cross would be an ideal opportunity to use some mathematics to determine the role of chance in your experiments. How traits pass into a sperm or egg cell is a matter of chance. Statistics is the branch of mathematics used to study probabilities. Consult the bibliography for references on statistics. Keep in mind that a statistical comparison has sometimes provided biologists with a clue that something unusual is happening in the way a trait is inherited. For example, you may find that two separate traits do not pass into a gamete simply by chance.

Another unusual situation may arise when the environment is changed. For instance, curly wings can be seen only when flies are kept at 25°C. At room temperature, the wings are straight like those of normal flies.

Examine other traits for sensitivity to temperature changes. Explore other environmental factors to see if a trait appears only under certain conditions. Experiment with various intensities of light, food additives, or changes in atmospheric pressure. If a change is noticed, determine whether heredity is involved by using the fly in genetic crosses. Does the trait appear in future generations when the environment is changed and then disappear when original conditions are reestablished?

One environmental factor almost guaranteed to cause a trait to change is radiation. Any change in the genetic information is called a mutation. Exposure to X-rays has been used to produce mutations in wing pat-

normal   mutant

Figure 23. A mutation accounts for the difference between the wings of normal (left) and mutant (right) fruit flies.

terns (see Figure 23) and eye colors of fruit flies. Contact a local hospital or university for use of their X-ray equipment to conduct a project on mutations. The technician must operate the equipment, but make sure to record the amount of radiation given to your flies. When you have identified an interesting mutation, use the fly in a genetic cross to study its pattern of inheritance.

Mutations can also be brought about by ultraviolet light and chemicals. Such chemicals are known as mutagens. Nitrous acid, DDT, formaldehyde, and mercury are known mutagens. Some chemicals used in food additives, weed killers, and insecticides are suspected mutagens. Conduct a project using fruit flies to confirm a suspected mutagen or identify a new one. Check with a local hospital or university to see if someone is studying the effects of mutagens. **This type of project must be done under the close supervision of a scientist working in this area.**

SEX PLAYS A ROLE

Some traits are linked to the sex of an individual. For example, white eyes in *Drosophila* are determined by a gene located on only one of the two sex chromosomes, known as the X chromosome. Carry out a project to study the inheritance of traits that are sex-linked. Cross white-eyed males with virgin, red-eyed females. Follow this trait over several generations. Based on its pattern of inheritance, plan a project to identify other sex-linked traits. Investigate whether such traits are more likely to mutate or be influenced by changes in the environment.

Eye color also provides information about another genetic pattern: nondisjunction. Normally the members of each chromosome pair separate when the sperm and egg are formed. In some situations, however, they fail to do so. As a result, a sex cell receives an extra chromosome. Certain results can come about only through nondisjunction. For example, a vermilion-eyed female produced by mating red-eyed males with virgin, vermilion-eyed females must be the result of nondisjunction. Check a biology textbook to understand why this must be the case. You can then undertake a project to identify another trait that results from nondisjunction.

Nondisjunction is a problem in humans resulting in Down's syndrome and other genetic diseases. You could make a significant contribution to genetic research by identifying an agent that reduces the chances of nondisjunction.

MAPPING GENES

Another contribution to genetics by fruit flies has been the ability to map the location of genes on chromosomes. If two genes are on the same chromosome, they stay together for the most part when the sperm and egg are formed. Such genes are said to be linked. Biologists could predict the outcome of crosses involving linked genes. But certain crosses of fruit flies led to unexpected results. Biologists could explain the origin of offspring from these crosses only by suggesting that at times, linked genes are exchanged between chromosomes (see Figure 24). By measuring the frequency of this exchange, scientists can determine the distance between two linked genes.

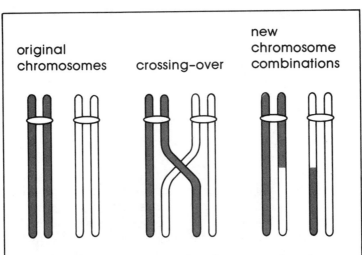

original chromosomes   crossing-over   new chromosome combinations

Figure 24. Chromosomes pair up, cross over, break, and rejoin to form new combinations of linked genes when sperm and egg cells are formed.

Chromosome maps are invaluable. Mapping makes it possible to tell which genes are located on a particular chromosome. Moreover, a detailed map provides the order and position of each gene on the chromosome. Such information is needed if a biologist wanted to remove a gene responsible for a disease or replace a defective gene with a functional one. A biologist could not do this without knowing where to look.

Biologists have developed detailed chromosome maps for *Drosophila* and many other organisms, including both plants and animals. Efforts are currently under way to map the chromosomes in humans using a variety of techniques. Although several hundred human genes have been mapped, the locations of thousands remain unknown. A significant contribution would be made by a project that adds just one gene to the human chromosome map.

Another method to map the location of genes stems

from the study of giant chromosomes. The chromosomes in the salivary glands of *Drosophila* keep dividing without separating. Consequently, they are quite large and have distinctive light and dark bands. The salivary glands can be removed and stained to see the banding patterns. These bands proved useful to biologists looking for particular genes.

For example, if a trait appeared at the same time a band puffed up and became more distinct, a biologist could make a connection between the trait and the location of the puff on the chromosome. Also, if something were wrong with a chromosome, such as a missing piece or unusual shape, any observable change in the fruit fly could be linked to that area of the chromosome. In effect, these giant chromosomes became another way of mapping genes.

Human chromosomes, on the other hand, are small. To study their banding patterns, biologists grow human cells in culture where they are treated with chemicals to make the chromosomes swell. If the cells are from a person with a disease or unusual trait, the bands can be compared to those in the chromosomes of a normal person. Any difference might pinpoint the location of the gene responsible for the disease or trait under study.

A rather sophisticated project would involve an attempt to culture cells from an animal or plant with an unusual trait. Treat the cells with a chemical to enlarge the chromosomes. Then check the banding patterns. Compare them to those in the chromosomes of an organism lacking the unusual trait. Look for enlarged puffs, missing pieces, broken-off ends, or extra segments on one of the chromosomes. If something unusual is present, you would have evidence linking the trait with a particular location on a chromosome.

BACTERIAL GENETICS

For many genetics projects, no organism may be better suited than bacteria. You can get more bacteria in a shorter time and smaller space than any plant or animal.

For example, the bacterium *Escherichia coli* doubles every 20 minutes. Billions of these bacterial cells can be grown in a flask containing some simple nutrients. With so many around, you might think finding an interesting specimen for a genetic study would be difficult. Not at all!

For instance, you can carry out a project to pick out just one type from all the others growing in a flask. Grow *E. coli* in a minimal medium (containing no food supplements) to which penicillin has been added. Most cells will grow, try to divide, but die because of the penicillin. Some, known as nutritional mutants, remain inactive in the minimal medium. In this state, the penicillin cannot kill them. The solution can be spun down in a centrifuge to separate the dead bacteria from the dormant but live ones.

The living bacteria are then plated on nutrient agar cultures where they become active, grow, and reproduce. These cells represent a clone of genetically identical bacteria. Examine how temperature changes, ultraviolet light, radiation, or mutagens affect the nutritional mutation. Expose the bacteria to any of these factors before growing them in the minimal media. Compare the number of bacterial colonies you obtain after the cells are transferred to nutrient agar. The more colonies found on nutrient agar, the greater the number of bacteria with the nutritional mutation. Identify both inhibitors and promotors of the mutation rate.

Manipulating the type of medium to study the genetics of bacteria is another possibility for a project. Suppose you had a bacterial strain that required the presence of a certain amino acid in the medium in order to grow. (By the way, many different types of bacteria and culture media are available from scientific supply companies.) Assume you had another strain that needed the addition of a different amino acid to grow. Mix both strains and grow them in a medium supplemented with both amino acids. Obviously, both strains can grow and reproduce. But what would happen if you took a sample of the two bacteria growing in the supplemented media and plated them on minimal media lacking *both* these amino acids? Logically, neither should grow.

Surprisingly, bacteria will grow. This is possible because genes have been transferred from one bacterial strain into the other, producing a new genetic strain (see Figure 25). These new bacteria are known as recombinants. In effect, they have undergone sexual reproduction by rearranging genes from two parents into a new combination that permits them to grow without either amino acid.

Design a project to produce a new strain by recombining the genetic material from two different types of bacteria. You can get ideas by checking what bacteria are commercially available. Or you can create your own interesting types by producing mutations with X-rays or chemicals. You will have to test for a nutritional mutation by growing the mutated bacteria on different media.

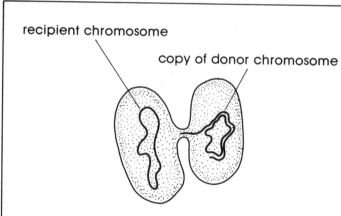

Figure 25. Genes can be exchanged between bacteria. The donor bacterium makes copies of the genes before they are transferred; only some may be exchanged before the two bacteria break apart from each other.

Perhaps your bacteria will need a particular amino acid, sugar, or vitamin added to the minimal medium in order to grow.

No matter how you get two nutritional mutations, each requiring a different additive to survive, grow them in a media supplemented with both additives. Then transfer some of these bacteria onto agar lacking both additives. Only recombinants will survive. Investigate how you can promote recombination between the bacteria: Vary the temperature, add different ingredients to the supplemented media, or grow the two strains in the presence of different sound frequencies.

THERE'S MORE TO THE STORY

As with all the other topics covered in this book, only a limited number of possible projects in a particular area can be covered. But genetics, perhaps more so than any other area in biology today, offers the greatest challenges and therefore the opportunity for so many projects. After all, with all due respect to the environment, an organism is a product of its genes. Most of what we know about genetics comes from studies with bacteria, yeast, and viruses. Biologists are busy using these organisms in projects aimed at adding to our knowledge of genetics.

To many, the most promising approach involves special techniques for inserting genes into organisms. These genes are obtained from different species or prepared by artificial means. To get the genes from another species, biologists must extract the hereditary material from the organism. This hereditary material consists of a chemical called deoxyribonucleic acid, abbreviated DNA.

If you want to extract some DNA, put a teaspoonful of baker's yeast in a mortar. Add three times as much sand and grind thoroughly with a pestle for 5 minutes to break open the cell walls of the yeast cells. Add 15 ml of 5% trichloroacetic acid and grind for another 5 minutes. Allow the sand to settle and carefully decant the solution into test tubes. Centrifuge for 5 minutes. Discard the supernatant (the liquid at the top) and stir the precipitate (the solid at the bottom) in 20 ml of 10% sodium chloride solution. Place this solution in a boiling water bath for 10 minutes. Allow the solution to cool and then centrifuge it for 3 minutes. Decant the supernatant into a clean test tube. Add two volumes of ethanol. Cool the solution in an ice bath; the DNA will precipitate as a white solid.

Centrifuge to collect this precipitate. Dissolve the solid in distilled water. To test for DNA, mix 3 ml of this solution with 6 ml of diphenylamine (also called Diche) reagent. Place the test tube in a boiling water bath for 30 minutes. Allow the solution to cool. A purplish or bluish color indicates the presence of DNA. Conduct a project to see if this DNA extraction procedure works with other organisms besides yeast. If you are unsuccessful, try modifying the procedure.

DNA extracted from an organism can then be used to insert foreign genes into bacteria. Such unnatural recombinants have been used to produce bacteria useful to humans. These genetically altered bacteria can produce insulin, growth hormones, and other beneficial products. Concerns have been raised about this gene manipulation, known as recombinant DNA technology. But the hope is that it will unravel many mysteries, including those concerning how genes function to turn a simple-looking fertilized egg cell into a fully formed adult. There are many questions to answer concerning the development of an adult organism from a simple beginning, as you will see in the next chapter.

7

DEVELOPMENT OF ANIMALS AND PLANTS

How does a simple, fertilized egg cell, known as a zygote, develop into a complex adult organism? Although biologists have investigated this question for hundreds of years, they still don't have all the answers. But they do have some understanding of a few processes that are part of development, beginning with the mechanisms involved in producing sperm and egg cells. In fact, biologists were able to predict something about this process even before they observed it for the first time.

Every organism has cells with a set number of chromosomes, remaining constant from one generation to the next. Your cells, with a few exceptions, contain 46 chromosomes. One exception is the egg and sperm cell. If each of these cells had 46 chromosomes, the zygote would have twice that number upon fertilization. This number would double every generation. In a relatively short time, an organism would be nothing more than a bag of chromosomes. Obviously, this is not what happens.

Biologists predicted that some process must occur to cut the chromosome number in half every time an egg or sperm is formed. When fertilization occurred, the original number would be restored. After making their prediction, biologists set about to find this process. They discovered that chromosomes did indeed get divided in half whenever sex cells were formed. Known as meiosis, this process reduces the chromosome number by half. Fertilization then restores the original number.

FERTILIZATION

Fertilization can be studied in a number of organisms. A most suitable one is the sea urchin, since its sperm and egg cells can be easily obtained without injury to the animal. In addition, since fertilization and development occur externally, these processes can be observed with a microscope.

Place a sea urchin mouth side up over a small beaker filled with seawater. Inject 1 ml of 0.5M potassium chloride solution into the soft tissues surrounding the mouth parts (see Figure 26). After a few minutes, the sex cells will be released through small pores on the bottom of the animal. Eggs will be yellowish or clear, while sperm will be white. Since you cannot sex a sea urchin by its external appearance, you may have to inject several before you find both sexes.

First, observe egg and sperm cells separately under a microscope. Then prepare a slide containing both cells for observation. Try to see the sperm swimming against the egg in an attempt to fertilize it. If fertilization occurs, a membrane will appear around the egg. The zygote will begin its journey to an adult in about 1 hour; at this time the zygote will divide to form two cells.

Carry out a project to observe the different stages of sea urchin development. Mix sperm and egg cells in a beaker of seawater. Maintain a constant temperature by suspending the beaker in an aquarium containing adult sea urchins. Remove samples at periodic intervals for microscopic observation. Be sure to change the seawater in the beaker every day to prevent contamination.

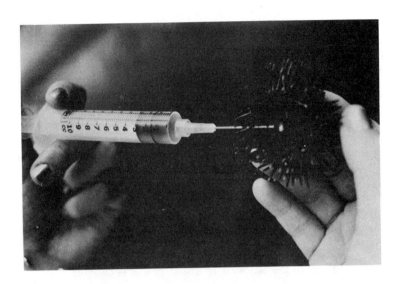

FIGURE 26. INJECTING A POTASSIUM CHLORIDE
SOLUTION INTO A SEA URCHIN WILL CAUSE THE
ANIMAL TO SHED ITS EGGS OR SPERM.

One of the first experiments done to study development involved placing some sea urchin embryos at the
two-cell stage into a small vial filled with seawater. The
embryos were gently shaken to separate the two cells.
Each cell was then carefully watched as it developed
into a normal, adult organism. The cells of sea urchin
embryos can also be separated at later stages of development by shaking them in calcium-free water. In some
cases, the top cells will separate from those on the bottom; in others, the cells on the left will be shaken loose
from those on the right (see Figure 27).

An interesting project would involve separating the
cells at different stages of development. Follow how
each develops. Replace the cells in seawater, stir gently,
and the cells will rearrange themselves into their normal
pattern. Vary the time the cells are separated to see
how this affects their ability to regroup. Based on your

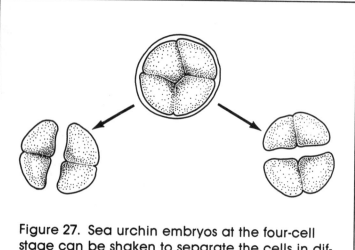

Figure 27. Sea urchin embryos at the four-cell stage can be shaken to separate the cells in different ways. Each fragment can be studied to see how it develops.

observations, arrive at some conclusion concerning the role of the nucleus, cytoplasm, and environment on animal development.

You can also investigate the effects of changing the temperature on both fertilization and development. Explore other ways to affect these processes: Vary the concentrations of sperm and egg cells, add chemicals to the seawater, or expose the zygotes to increasing doses of radiation or ultraviolet light. Freeze egg and sperm cells and check their ability to undergo fertilization after thawing. Develop a method of freezing that maintains a high viability of these sex cells.

Sea urchins are sometimes difficult to obtain, especially if you don't live near the ocean or if you decide to begin your project in the middle of winter. In that case, you can study the development of frogs. Frogs are easier to obtain, even in winter. From October until April, each female frog contains about 2,000 eggs. In the spring, environmental conditions are just right to trigger the release of her eggs, which will be fertilized externally.

How changes in the environment cause the female to shed her eggs is not completely understood. Both water temperature and amount of sunlight are known to be important. Biologists have implicated the pineal gland, a small lobe of the brain, as being responsible for detecting the amount of light present. In effect, the pineal gland acts as a biological timekeeper, not only in frogs but also in many other animals, possibly even humans. Design a project to shed some light on the role of the pineal gland in animal development.

If you're planning a project on frog development, don't try to find a frog carrying mature eggs every time you need one. Instead, you can inject a pituitary preparation into a female's abdomen. Within 48 hours, you can check for eggs by grasping the female and gently squeezing her abdomen. The eggs will pour out when they are ready (see Figure 28). Removing the pituitary

FIGURE 28. GENTLY SQUEEZING THE ABDOMEN OF A GRAVID FEMALE WILL FORCE OUT THE MATURE EGGS.

glands to prepare the hormone injection is quite difficult. A simpler way is to order a frog ovulation kit, complete with pituitary extract, syringe, frogs, and instructions, from a scientific supply company. Directions for obtaining the sperm and fertilizing the eggs are included.

Frog embryos have the ability to develop over a wide temperature range, although the rate of development varies. Compare this rate with changes in temperature. An interesting project would be a comparative study: Is sea urchin or frog development affected more by a certain chemical, level of ultraviolet light, or temperature variation?

Frog embryos are also useful in a project designed to study the effects of hormones on development. If fertilization is successful, try to maintain your embryos until they develop into tadpoles. You can investigate the effects of various hormones on tadpoles as they develop into adult frogs. Try different concentrations of thyroid hormones on culture dishes containing tadpoles. Experiment with both thyroxin and triiodothyronine to see if one is more effective in promoting development. Although many of the changes are internal and therefore not visible, you can measure the rate of development by observing some external features. As tadpoles develop, the tail will shorten and disappear, both forelimbs and hindlimbs will form, and the body shape will resemble that of an adult frog.

CHICKENS

The chicken egg has been used to study development for over 300 years. It owes its popularity to its availability and size. Like all eggs, a chicken egg is a single cell, with its large size the result of all the yolk stored to feed the developing chick.

All you need to conduct a project on chick development are some fertilized eggs and an incubator (see Figure 29). Careful control of both temperature and humidity is necessary for normal development. The eggs must be rotated several times a day to prevent the embryos

FIGURE 29. AN INCUBATOR MAINTAINS BOTH
THE PROPER TEMPERATURE AND HUMIDITY
REQUIRED FOR NORMAL CHICK DEVELOPMENT.

from sticking to the shell as they develop. By the way, you have to get the eggs from a scientific supply company or a farmer. Those sold in supermarkets are not fertilized since roosters are not allowed in the hen house!

Observe a chick as it develops by opening a window in the egg. To make the window, lay the egg horizontally in a nest of towels crumpled in a finger bowl. Allow the egg to remain undisturbed so that the embryo floats to the top. Use a fine pointed needle to scratch a rectangular area smaller than a glass cover slip on the egg's surface. Break away small pieces of the shell with a forceps until the embryo is exposed (see Figure 30). Use a dissecting microscope or hand lens for closer observation.

After making a window in an egg, you can seal it by positioning a cover slip over the opening and then closing off any spaces with wax. Be careful since any hot wax

FIGURE 30. USE A FINE-POINTED NEEDLE AND
FORCEPS TO OPEN A "WINDOW" IN A FERTILIZED
EGG TO OBSERVE HOW THE CHICK DEVELOPS.

dripped into the egg will kill the embryo. You can observe the chick develop through the glass window or remove it when necessary.

Carry out a project to study chick development. One day after fertilization, the embryo appears as a tiny white spot near the surface. In 14 days, feathers on the wings and legs will be visible. In 21 days, the chick will hatch. Note when other structures begin to appear. Look for the development of four extraembryonic membranes, not present in sea urchins or frogs. Compare chick development with those of other birds whose eggs are available. Make a record of similarities and differences.

Chick eggs serve as a good medium for growing different kinds of organisms, including viruses. Experiment with different organisms to see which ones can use a chick egg for its own development.

Chick eggs are also ideal vehicles for studying the effects of various chemical and physical treatments on animal development. Inject different chemicals into an egg. Test the effects of different dosages. Care should be taken to use only sterile solutions since any microorganisms introduced by injection will grow rapidly and kill the embryo. After injecting the egg, observe the embryo for any abnormalities in development. Determine at which age the chick is most sensitive to the chemical.

Physical treatments can include increased atmospheric pressure, ultrasonic vibrations, radiation, or mild centrifugation to increase gravitational forces. You may find it easier to conduct a project on chick development by working with eggs before the embryo has taken on its adult appearance. If you don't wish to conduct a project on chick embryos of any age, wait until they hatch. Then undertake a feeding project. Prepare different types of chick feed mixtures. Record the weights over a period of time to determine which feed is best for their growth and development. You might discover a combination useful to chicken farmers.

REGENERATION

Many animals may develop normally, only to lose a part of their body because of a predator or accident. Some are able to replace or regenerate this lost part. For years, fishermen cut up starfish and tossed them back into the sea, thinking they were eliminating these shellfish predators. But the fishermen were unaware of the starfish's ability to regenerate lost parts. Consequently, there were more starfish than ever before to prey on the clams and oysters!

Cut up a starfish to obtain the smallest piece capable of regenerating an entire organism. Determine if a starfish can regenerate two lost arms as quickly as one. Remove all the arms, leaving only the central disc. Does this disc regenerate an entire organism? Observe each arm to see if it forms a complete starfish. Cut half off one arm and two-thirds off another. Compare the rate of regeneration in both arms.

Increase the temperature, vary the salt composition of the water, expose the regenerating parts to a magnetic field, or pass a mild electric current through the seawater to study changes in the rate of regeneration. Check on safety factors if you decide to pass an electric current through water.

If starfish prove too cumbersome to work with, you can develop a project to study regeneration with the help of a freshwater flat worm called planaria (see Figure 31). Planaria can be maintained in filtered pond water. Tap water that has sat for several days to eliminate the chlorine is also suitable. Use a sharp razor blade or scalpel to make your cuts. Use your imagination to make various types of cuts. Study the regenerative properties of each piece. Don't feed regenerating planaria, and change the water daily. Keep them in a cool, dark place.

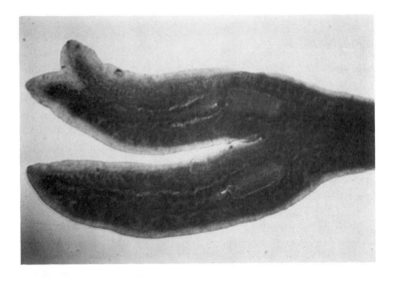

FIGURE 31. *PLANARIA*, A FRESHWATER FLATWORM, IS AN EXCELLENT SPECIMEN FOR A NUMBER OF BIOLOGY PROJECTS, INCLUDING A STUDY OF FACTORS INVOLVED IN REGENERATION. THIS PLANARIA IS REGENERATING TWO HEADS.

Determine the smallest piece that can regenerate a new head or tail. If your cuts do not completely sever the animal, you can produce some interesting combinations: a planaria with three heads, or two tails, or even one with three heads *and* two tails. Sometimes the separated pieces will rejoin and heal. In this case, you will have to cut them again or keep them separated in some way.

Investigate the effects of ultraviolet light and chemicals such as colchicine, nicotine, and adrenalin on the rate of regeneration. Pass an electric current through the water as the planaria regenerate. If you discover something that has a significant effect, test its ability to influence the regenerative ability of an animal that cannot replace lost parts.

PLANTS

A colorful flower garden can be the source for several projects on plant development. Did you realize that flowers are the reproductive organs of plants? But unlike the reproductive structures of animals, which are permanent, flowers have a limited life span. After fertilization, most flower parts die and drop from the plant; some remain to become part of the fruit.

Before the flowers begin to die, collect as many different kinds as possible. An interesting project would be a comparison study. Make note of each flower's color, fragrance, and structural details. Check the bibliography for a reference to help you identify all the parts. Include microscopic observations, especially on pollen grains, as part of your comparison. Describe both similarities and differences between your specimens. Classify each plant as monocot or dicot, complete or incomplete, primitive or advanced, and monoecious or dioecious.

Monocots have their floral parts in groups of three or multiples of threes; dicots have theirs in groups of four or five or multiples of these. A flower having all parts is complete; one missing a part is called incomplete. Primitive plants show radial symmetry (a circular pattern); more advanced ones have bilateral (left and right) or irregular symmetry. A monoecious plant has either male or female reproductive structures; a dioecious one has both sexes as part of the same flower.

If you prefer to concentrate on just one flowering plant, your project may include a thorough description of its life history. Our knowledge of plants is limited to those of economic importance, ones used either as a food source or nursery stock. Much remains to be discovered about the others.

Select a wildflower. Compile a detailed account of one year in its life cycle. Describe changes in its appearance, methods of reproduction, interactions with other organisms, and patterns of growth. Include measurements. Keep records of leaf size, plant height, and root depth throughout the year. Investigate crossing the plant with other species to produce hybrids. Determine any commercial value of your original plant or hybrid.

SEEDS

Development in flowering plants begins with a seed. The seed consists of the embryo, stored food, and the seed coat. Soak some seeds in water overnight, cut them in half with a sharp razor blade, and observe them under a microscope. Make a microscopic comparison of different seeds. Identify the various parts by referring to a book on plants. Determine if starch is present by covering the cut seed in Lugol's iodine.

Besides starch, the seeds of some flowering plants have been shown to contain substances similar to antibiotics. Design a project to detect such a substance. One way would involve spreading bacteria onto nutrient agar and then placing cut seeds on these plates. A clear area free of microorganisms near the seed would indicate the presence of an antimicrobial agent. Check the effectiveness of this substance against different types of bacteria. The next step would be to isolate the substance and identify its chemical nature. Determine if the seeds could be an economical source for the antimicrobial chemical.

A project to study plant development could be undertaken with germinating seeds. Wrap some soaked seeds in paper towels. Fasten the roll with a rubber band and place the towel with the seeds at the top end into a beaker of water (see Figure 32). Unroll the towel whenever you wish to examine the extent of germination. Replace the seeds in the beaker for further development.

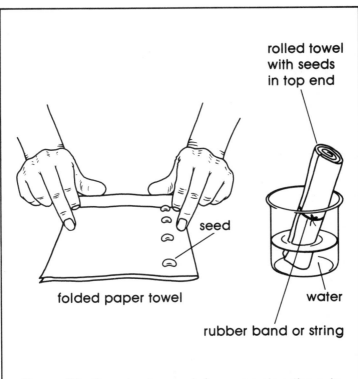

rolled towel
with seeds
in top end

seed

folded paper towel

water

rubber band or string

Figure 32. Germinate seeds by wrapping them in a paper towel half submerged in a beaker of water. Be sure the seeds are in the half that extends above the water.

Compare germination rates of different seeds. Investigate factors that can affect germination. Prepare a solution for soaking the paper towels that will double the rate of germination. You may also want to experiment with factors that will postpone germination. The seeds of most plants require a period of dormancy before they germinate. If they germinate and then encounter unfavorable environmental conditions, the seeds will stop growing and die. Farmers may want to keep seeds dormant longer than usual for such circumstances.

By the way, biologists are experimenting with growing plants without soil by placing them in solutions supplemented with nutrients. This type of plant development is called hydroponics. Conduct an experiment in hydroponics to grow a vegetable or fruit. Develop solutions to grow crop plants that produce greater yields under hydroponic conditions.

PLANT HORMONES

Plant development depends on several hormones, including auxin, cytokinin, gibberellin, ethylene, abscisic acid, and florigen. Auxin influences a plant's response to light and gravity, inhibits the formation of lateral buds, and promotes fruit development. Cytokinin stimulates cell division and growth. Gibberellin helps the stem to grow tall. Ethylene speeds fruit ripening. Abscisic acid is involved in dormancy. Florigen is a hypothetical hormone thought to play a role in flowering.

Actually, each plant hormone has more functions, some of which are not clearly understood. Biologists believe a hormone is involved in flower production but have been unable to isolate one. They also have evidence indicating hormones are used by plants to measure the length of day. They are also unsure of the effects of exposing developing plants to different combinations of hormones.

In short, plant hormones leave many questions to be answered and therefore offer numerous possibilities for a project. If you are interested in exploring this area, check the bibliography for additional information on plant hormones.

WHEN YOU'RE AN ADULT

If all proceeds normally, the zygote and seed develop into adult organisms, complete with systems that work together to keep them functioning, regardless of changes in the environment. The next chapter will look at these various systems and suggest ideas for projects that can add to our knowledge of their role in the adult organism.

8

SYSTEMS IN
LIVING THINGS

As you have seen, an organism develops from a simple cell into a complex adult. When development is complete, the adult form of most plants and animals consists of different tissues, which are groups of cells similar in structure and function. In turn, tissues are assembled to form organs, such as a leaf, stem, stomach, heart, lung, kidney, or brain. Several organs function together to make up a system, such as the digestive, circulatory, respiratory, excretory, and nervous systems. The adult organism depends on the proper functioning of all its systems in order to survive. These systems offer much to explore and present many possibilities for a biology project.

DIGESTION

In organisms made up of many cells, digestion refers to the breakdown of food materials into smaller pieces so that they can be absorbed and used by the individual cells. The digestive process actually involves two stages: breakdown of food substances while they are still outside the organism and absorption of the smaller particles into each cell where they are broken down even further. The former process is called extracellular digestion, the latter is known as intracellular digestion.

Carry out a project on extracellular digestion. Begin by placing several hydras in a watch glass filled approximately halfway with water. Observe them with a dissecting microscope. Wait until they are extended and relaxed (see Figure 33). Place several specimens of *Daphnia* near the hydra's tentacles and observe what happens. Make sketches as the hydra uses its tentacles to capture a daphnia. Observe what happens to the daphnia as the hydra begins the process of extracellular digestion. Design an experiment to determine how the hydra detected the daphnia: Was it visual, tactile, or chemical?

Specialized cells in the hydra known as nematocysts release a poisoned barb to paralyze and kill its prey. Prepare a wet mount of a hydra that has captured a daph-

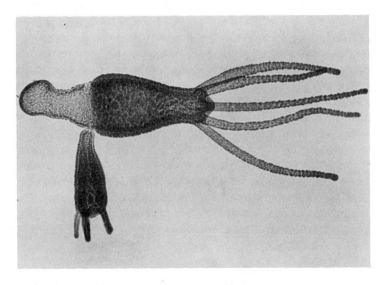

FIGURE 33. *HYDRA*, A FRESHWATER ORGANISM FOUND IN PONDS AND STREAMS, EXTENDS ITS TENTACLES TO TRAP ITS PREY.

nia and examine it under a phase-contrast microscope to observe discharged nematocysts. Addition of acetic acid will also cause the nematocysts to discharge. Determine where the nematocysts are concentrated on the hydra. Investigate other ways of activating the nematocysts. Add various salts to the water, alter the light intensity, change the temperature, or test the effects of chemicals found in your biology lab. Determine if a hydra discharges additional nematocysts if it is in the process of eating.

Experiment with ways of preventing the discharge of nematocysts, even when food is present. Use a sharp scalpel to remove some of the tentacles. Add poisons, metals, alcohol, or aspirin to the water. Investigate what other kinds of animals hydras eat. Check if any plants or microorganisms such as yeast produce a feeding response. Based on your results, what can you conclude about extracellular digestion in a hydra?

A number of different animals are suitable for studying extracellular digestion: planaria, sea urchins, snails, earthworms, crayfish, fiddler crabs, and barnacles. Compare the various methods of extracellular digestion used by these organisms. Include a study of food preferences. Present each organism with a variety of foods. Allow sufficient time for a response. Be sure to test each food sample with a sufficient number of organisms. Compare living to dead food samples. Test the effect of freezing on the attractiveness of food. Experiment with food materials having strong odors or vibrant colors.

You may be surprised to learn that some plants, including the Venus flytrap, sundew, and pitcher plants, carry out extracellular digestion. Known as carnivorous plants, they secrete enzymes to digest insects, worms, and even larger animals including birds and frogs. These plants are usually found in acidic soils where nitrogen is in low supply. Biologists believe these plants compensate for the lack of nitrogen in the soil by obtaining it from their prey.

Tiny electrodes placed in the tentacles extending from sundew leaves have detected electrical activity when the plant comes in contact with an insect. These studies indicate that electrical impulses, much like those sent through the nerves of animals, close the leaves to trap the insect. Biologists suspect that carnivorous plants may use electrical signals to coordinate other processes besides digestion. Design a project to explore the mechanisms used by other carnivorous plants to trap their prey. Investigate whether such mechanisms are used for other plant activities.

Whether in animals or plants, extracellular digestion depends upon the release of enzymes. You may recall that the three major classes of organic compounds in foods are carbohydrates, lipids, and proteins. Organisms secrete enzymes to digest these compounds. Investigate the interaction between digestive enzymes and food materials. You can use saliva to digest carbohydrates, pancreatin for lipids, and pepsin for proteins.

Vary the size of the food particles. Use different concentrations of enzymes. Alter the temperature and acidity of the solutions. Investigate the effect of adding bile salts. Test for the products of digestion. Explore various animals and plants for the presence of digestive enzymes. For example, cut up some planaria or plants into small pieces. Mix the pieces with water and sand in a mortar and grind thoroughly to make a paste. Filter and test the liquid for the presence of digestive enzymes. Undertake a comparative study to see if changes in pH and temperature have the same effect on digestive enzymes isolated from different organisms.

You can study intracellular digestion by using specimens of *Paramecium*. Add some water and Congo red powder to a package of yeast. Boil the solution for 5 minutes. Then prepare a wet mount after mixing the yeast and paramecia. Use the highest magnification of a microscope to observe what happens to the yeast particles as they are ingested by the paramecia. Follow the path of the yeast as they are digested inside the cell. See what other food materials you can get *Paramecium* to eat. Experiment with ways of inhibiting intracellular digestion.

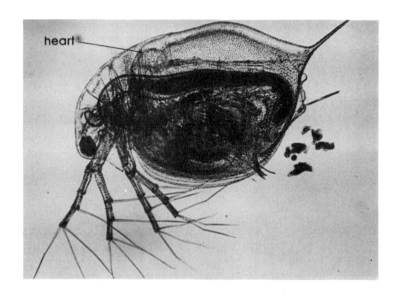

heart

FIGURE 34. DAPHNIA ARE USEFUL FOR A PROJECT
INVESTIGATING FACTORS THAT AFFECT HEART ACTION.

CIRCULATION

Besides feeding them to hydra, you can use *Daphnia* for
a project investigating factors that affect heartbeat
rate. *Daphnia's* heart can easily be seen under the low
power of a microscope (see Figure 34). Place some
daphnia in a small drop of petroleum jelly on a depression slide. After positioning the coverslip, count the number of heartbeats for 15 seconds and multiply by 4 to get
the rate per minute. Calculate an average based on at
least five counts. Explore environmental changes on the
action of the heart: Vary the temperature; add different
chemicals, especially ethanol, nicotine, caffeine, tran-
quilizers, and over-the-counter drugs; and alter the salt
and carbon dioxide content of the water.

An interesting organism for a project on heartbeat is
a tunicate, commonly known as a sea squirt. Of all animals using a pumping organ to circulate fluids, only the

tunicate heart is known to reverse itself and alternate the flow of blood. Use a dissecting microscope to observe this reversal. Waves of contraction will sweep over the heart in one direction for a minute or two, and then change direction. Work out a procedure to change this rhythm. Can you manipulate the sea squirt's environment so that the heart will not reverse its pattern of beating?

The effects of environmental changes can also be the basis for a project investigating the rate of circulation in an animal. Place a goldfish between two wads of cotton soaked in water. Place its tail between two glass slides and then put the fish in a petri dish (see Figure 35). Scan the tail area under a low-power objective lens until you can see blood flowing through a capillary. Experiment with ways of affecting the rate of blood flow. Keep the tail moist. Don't keep the fish out of water for more than 5 minutes.

Conduct a comparative study to include changes in the blood flow of other animals. You could use sea star, sea urchins, or sea cucumbers. Allow the animal to attach itself to a glass slide. Place the animal in sea water and position the tube feet for observation with a dissecting microscope. The blood circulates down one side of the tube foot and up the other.

For any organism to survive, the blood must circulate freely and move through the body with a steady flow. Interference with blood flow can lead to a heart attack or stroke. Hardening of the arteries caused by fat accumulation, known as atherosclerosis, contributes to both heart attacks and strokes. The causes of atherosclerosis are not completely understood. High cholesterol levels, cigarette smoking, and high blood pressure are associated with atherosclerosis. Certain foods, female hormones, and exercise seem to protect against atherosclerosis. Using an organism where you can see the blood flow, design a project to investigate possible ways of preventing atherosclerosis.

A number of different substances are carried by the blood as it flows through an organism. In humans, blood consists of red cells, white cells, platelets, and plasma.

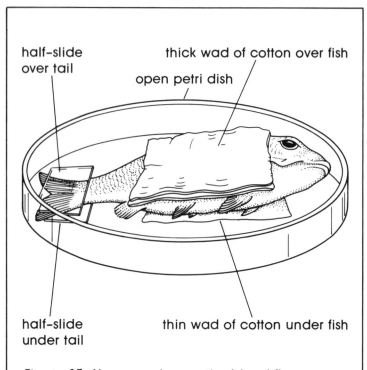

half-slide over tail

thick wad of cotton over fish

open petri dish

half-slide under tail

thin wad of cotton under fish

Figure 35. You can observe the blood flow through the capillaries of a goldfish. Place the tail between two glass slides and keep the goldfish moist with cotton soaked with water. Don't keep the goldfish out of water for more than 5 minutes.

Plasma is 90% water. The remaining 10% is mostly made up of proteins used for clotting and fighting infections. A centrifuge can be used to separate blood into its various components.

Obtain a blood sample from an animal and place it in a centrifuge tube containing a small amount of sodium citrate. Stopper the tube and gently mix the contents;

the sodium citrate will prevent the blood from clotting. Centrifuge gently for 2 or 3 minutes. Remove the tube without disturbing the contents and place it in a rack. Measure the height of the red cell fraction and that of the plasma. Ignore the white cell fraction since it is too small to measure.

Calculate the hematocrit for the blood sample by dividing the height of the red blood cell fraction by the *total* height of the blood sample. Multiply by 100 to change to a percent. Repeat the procedure every other day for several weeks to detect any changes in the hematocrit. Experiment with ways of causing the hematocrit to change—can you increase the red blood cell fraction or change the percentage of plasma? Compare hematocrit results for different animals.

If you have blood available for hematocrits, use the opportunity to prepare blood smears for microscopic observation. Use a glass slide to spread a thin layer of blood on a second slide. For the best results, you must have a single layer of cells. Allow the blood to dry and then add a few drops of Wright's stain. After staining for 3 minutes, rinse with tap water, allow to dry, and observe the cells with the high-power objective lens.

Red blood cells will be purplish, while white blood cells will have a clear or bluish cytoplasm and a purplish nucleus. You may see several different types of white blood cells, based on the appearance of their nuclei. Refer to a biology textbook for help in identifying each type. Prepare blood smears from different animals to compare the cell types found in each.

Circulation of materials is a concern not only for animals but also for plants. Biologists are still unsure how plants transport materials, especially to such great heights as found in the giant redwoods. A number of different factors are believed to be involved, including the pressure exerted by roots. To study root pressure, hollow out a carrot, which is actually a root, with a cork borer and fill the hole with molasses. Insert a piece of glass tubing into a one-hole rubber stopper so that it extends into the molasses. Place the stopper in the carrot and submerge it in a beaker of water. Pressure exerted by the carrot will cause the molasses to rise in the tube. Experiment with ways of changing the rate at which the liquid rises in the tubing. Compare the results with the pressure exerted by other roots.

RESPIRATION

Several possibilities for projects on respiration were discussed in Chapter 4. As you may recall, respiration is the chemical process used by organisms to produce energy, usually with the use of oxygen and the release of carbon dioxide. Breathing is the mechanical process by which oxygen and carbon dioxide are exchanged between the organism and environment. Breathing rates can be studied in a number of organisms, including fish.

Observe a fish in an aquarium without disturbing it. Determine its breathing rate by counting the number of times the fish opens and closes its gill covers to pump water containing oxygen over the gills. Explore ways of changing the fish's rate of breathing: Increase the water temperature or salinity, change the acidity of the aquarium, or add different chemicals to the tank. Determine whether variations exist in different species. Experiment with both fresh- and saltwater fish.

Count the number of breaths you take in 1 minute. Do this after resting and performing different exercises. Place a paper bag over your nose and mouth. Breathe into the bag for 1 minute. Remove the bag and immediately count the number of breaths you take in 1 minute. Compare breathing patterns among your classmates. Include anyone who performs aerobic exercises. This type of exercising increases the amount of blood and oxygen carried by the hemoglobin. Consequently, a person who does aerobic exercises should be better able to reestablish their normal breathing pattern after performing some vigorous activity. Conduct a project to see which type of aerobic exercise is most effective as judged by measuring a person's breathing pattern.

You may be surprised to learn that oxygen can be harmful and even lethal to some organisms. For instance, certain bacteria are killed in the presence of oxygen. Even those organisms who need oxygen to live often suffer harmful side effects if oxygen pressure is too high. These effects include abnormal growth patterns, paralysis, even death. Undertake a project to study the effects of increased oxygen pressure on organisms. Insects are suitable for this study. You will need a sealed chamber capable of keeping both an increased gas pressure and a temperature range between 25°C and 30°C. Connect tanks of compressed oxygen, nitrogen, and air with pressure gauges to the chamber. Be sure to work under proper supervision since care should be taken when using gases under pressure. Your study may have some useful application for deep-sea divers and pilots who are exposed to varying oxygen pressures.

EXCRETION

An organism must excrete a number of waste products, including carbon dioxide, water, and nitrogen-containing substances. Since this last waste product is extremely poisonous, as much as possible must be eliminated. Aquatic organisms secrete nitrogen waste products in the form of ammonia; all birds and insects excrete them as uric acid; mammals largely eliminate them as urea.

Use goldfish for a project on excretion in an aquatic organism. You will have to decapitate a goldfish, open its abdomen, and remove its digestive system. The kidneys will be found as two brownish masses next to the spinal cord. Remove the kidneys and place them in a dish filled with Ringer's solution. Carefully tease the tissue apart to separate the tiny fibers; these are the kidney tubules.

Place some of the tubules in a dish and add several drops of phenol red. After 15 minutes, observe the tubules under low-power magnification. Because of active transport, the kidney tubules should be darker in color since they are taking up the dye from the surrounding fluid. Find out what factors affect the ability of these tubules to carry out active transport. Vary the conditions of the aquarium for a period of time, and then check the effect on active transport in the kidney tubules of the goldfish.

Excretion in insects can be studied with the help of earthworms. Anesthetize an earthworm after injecting it with a stain such as methylene blue. Dissect open its excretory system, consisting of tubules known as nephridia found along both sides of the earthworm (see Figure 36). The stain should help you locate the nephridia. Remove a few for observation under a dissecting microscope. Look for any signs of movement of the cilia, hairlike projections that beat in rhythm to move the waste products to the outside of the body. Design a project to explore excretion in the earthworm. Use the movement of the cilia as an indication of excretory action.

In mammals, the main excretory organ is the kidney. The kidney operates according to the principle of negative feedback. If the concentration of a certain substance gets too high, the excess is eliminated. On the other hand, if the concentration falls too low, the kidney switches gears to conserve as much as possible until the level is brought back within the normal range.

Refer to a biology textbook for the details of the kidney's structure. For a project demonstrating its operation, design a working model that operates on the principle of negative feedback. Recall that dialysis tubing mimics the function of cell membranes. A sophisticated model would actually monitor levels of substances and respond to fluctuations in their concentrations. Before building your model, you may want to contact a hospital to see how a dialysis machine works as a substitute for damaged or diseased kidneys.

THE NERVOUS SYSTEM

The nervous system is responsible for detecting and responding to stimuli, including light, odors, sounds, and touch. Carry out a project to determine to what extent

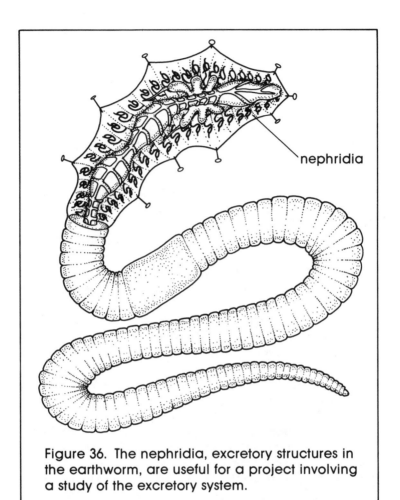

nephridia

Figure 36. The nephridia, excretory structures in the earthworm, are useful for a project involving a study of the excretory system.

various organisms respond to these stimuli. For example, check whether a planaria prefers the light or dark, avoids chemicals that emit odors, curls up when touched, or reacts to vibrations. Vary the intensity of the different stimuli to see if the planaria can detect these changes in its environment. Proceed with a different organism. Compile a list of organisms tested, stimuli used, and responses detected. Can you make any conclusion that applies to all organisms tested? Pay particular attention to any unusual responses.

Plan a project to check the ability of your classmates to respond to stimuli. Check their sensation of taste by dipping a small wad of cotton wrapped around a toothpick into various solutions, including vinegar, salt, sugar, and quinine water. Apply the solution to a small area of the tongue. Test various areas of the tongue to determine where each taste is detected. Vary the concentrations of each solution to determine the threshold of taste. Determine if any patterns of taste exist among your classmates.

Next, check for your classmates' ability to detect cold and heat, using pins that have been soaked in either ice or hot water. After drying it off, check to make sure the pin is not too hot. Touch different areas on the back of the hand to determine the location of hot and cold receptors. Pressure receptors can be located by inserting two pins into a wooden cork. Space the pins 2 cm apart from each other. Gently touch your subject's wrist in several places. Ask your subject how many pins are felt. Keep moving the pins in the cork closer together until your subject feels both pins as one. Record this distance for each person and compare the results.

Some people possess extrasensory perception, or ESP. A number of tests can be given to people to determine if they have any ESP powers. If you want to do a project on ESP, several kits for testing people are available from scientific supply companies.

Some people have the ability to change certain biological processes normally beyond conscious control. For example, these people can control their heartbeat rate, patterns of waves emitted by the brain, or secretion of digestive enzymes and hormones. Much remains to be discovered about this power, known as biofeedback. Application of biofeedback offers some interesting possibilities. A person with high blood pressure may learn how to control it to a certain extent, or someone suffering from migraine headaches may be able to relax muscles to relieve the tension.

Plan a project investigating biofeedback. Work under the proper supervision if your project involves human subjects. You could design and construct the equipment for such a project, or you can order various instruments from a scientific supply company. Determine the percentage of people who possess this ability. Conduct a long-term study to see if people can learn biofeedback control. Investigate what biological processes can be controlled through biofeedback. Explore if biofeedback exists in animals other than humans.

Biofeedback may turn out to be another way for humans to exert some degree of control over their biological world. In the past, we have used our knowledge of genetics to produce entire populations of plants and animals for various purposes. In effect, humans have controlled the evolutionary process of these organisms. You will next explore how the genes in populations change, by either natural or artificial means.

9

POPULATIONS AND EVOLUTION

Organisms of the same species living together in the same location are known as a population. Provided with unlimited food, space, and resources and protected from all predators, the size of a population would increase at a phenomenal rate. For example, a single *E. coli* bacterial cell, dividing every 20 minutes, would produce 72 generations weighing about 3 million kg in just 24 hours! Obviously, this massive growth does not occur. In nature, the growth of a population is controlled by a number of factors; limited food supply, presence of predators, disease, and lack of sufficient water are just a few examples.

You can carry out a project on population growth by working with yeast. Add half a package of dried yeast to 500 ml of light molasses and 500 ml of distilled water. Swirl the solution to disperse the yeast. After 30 minutes, take one drop, prepare a wet mount, and count the number of cells with a hemocytometer. Calculate the number of yeast cells per milliliter of solution. Place the yeast culture on a shaker to aerate the solution and keep the cells dispersed. Repeat your cell counts every day for 2 weeks.

Graph your results. Based on the shape of your graph, make as many conclusions as possible regarding the growth of the yeast population. Investigate ways of affecting the growth pattern: Vary the temperature, change the proportion of water and molasses, increase the acidity of the growth media, or add paramecia to prey upon the yeast.

If you prefer a larger organism for a project on population growth, use *Drosophila*. Place one pair consisting of a male and female fly in a culture vial. Prepare other vials, varying the number of mating pairs placed in each. After 7 days, discard the adults and count the number of larvae and pupae in each vial. The larvae and pupae are two stages in *Drosophila* development (see Figure 37). Also count the number of adult flies in each vial to determine the percentage of larvae that complete development. Experiment with ways to establish optimum conditions for population growth.

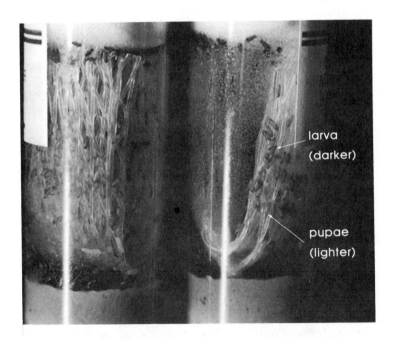

FIGURE 37. THE LARVAE AND PUPAE OF *DROSOPHILA*
DEVELOP ON THE SIDES OF THE CULTURE VIALS.

Compare different species of fruit flies to see if they differ in the way their populations grow. Some species undergo rapid population explosions, producing swarms of flies that have destroyed crops. Information about their growth patterns might be useful in attempting to control their destructive power.

Drosophila are also suitable for a project investigating the genetic advantage of certain organisms within a population. In the simplest situation, a trait is controlled by a pair of genetic factors. The members of this pair may be identical, in which case the individual is said to be homozygous for the trait. On the other hand, the factors may be different from each other, making the organism heterozygous for the trait. Genetic studies have indicated heterozygous individuals sometimes have an advantage in nature. This can be determined by comparing the number of offspring produced by heterozygous and homozygous individuals.

Obtain flies homozygous for a trait from a scientific supply company. If you mate flies homozygous for the dominant trait with ones homozygous for the recessive trait, then their offspring will be heterozygous. Use these flies in matings to see which type produces more offspring, especially under unfavorable conditions. If the heterozygous flies show superiority, manipulate their environment to reduce their reproductive advantage.

Heterozygous individuals have also been shown to be superior in plant populations. In the 1930s, two different corn strains were crossed to produce the heterozygous variety used for food today. This heterozygous corn is larger and hardier than either of the homozygous strains, proving economically beneficial to farmers. Conduct a project to produce either a plant or animal population that possesses genetic superiority in the heterozygous condition.

Whether you use flies, corn, or any other organism, any time you select particular individuals to mate, you are in control. In effect, you are selecting the genes that will be passed on to future generations. If you think about it, you'll realize that many people perform this selection process; some even do it for a living. For instance, animal breeders will select certain animals to mate to produce offspring with desirable traits: race horses with stronger leg muscles, Labrador retrievers with a keener sense of smell, or Siamese cats with smoother and more attractive coats. Plant breeders use the same method to produce crops that grow faster or plants with unusual floral patterns.

This process of choosing individual organisms to mate is called artificial selection. The purpose is to produce desired changes in future populations. Whenever a population changes with the passage of time, it has undergone the process of evolution. Charles Darwin, who proposed a theory on how evolution occurs, recognized the significance of artificial selection. An expert on raising and breeding pigeons, Darwin began his book *The Origin of Species* with a chapter on artificial selection.

Darwin expanded his ideas to explain how populations evolve without human intervention. He called his theory natural selection. Like artificial selection, only certain organisms are likely to survive and reproduce; others are more likely to die, failing to leave any survivors. Those that manage to produce offspring pass their traits on to future generations. Obviously, those that die cannot. Over a period of time, the makeup of the population would change, perhaps even producing one so different that it could be called a new species.

You might think a project involving evolution would not be feasible. After all, you read how changes in populations appear over a long period of time—time you don't have for your project. But such a project is possible, with the help of a little mathematics known as the Hardy-Weinberg principle. These two scientists used a model population exempt from any factors that would cause it to change or evolve. In effect, the genes in such a population are said to be in equilibrium. In order to be in equilibrium, Hardy and Weinberg stated that the population must be free of selection forces, mutations, mating preferences, and migration. Obviously, no population meets these conditions. If this is the case, then what is the usefulness of the Hardy-Weinberg principle?

This principle provides a reference point. The further

away from this point, the more the population has evolved. With the use of the Hardy-Weinberg principle, you can also be specific about what is happening to certain types of individuals in the population under study. You can also make predictions about what should happen to the population—will a certain type of organism become more common while another one disappears?

Check the bibliography for a reference explaining the mathematics involved in the Hardy-Weinberg principle. Don't worry if you're not good at math; the steps are easy to follow, requiring only some simple multiplication. Once you understand the math, you can easily analyze several human traits to see if the population in your school or town is evolving for the genes involved.

Obtain a piece of phenylthiocarbamide (PTC) paper and chew it just like gum. You'll soon discover if you are a taster—PTC produces a bitter taste for those who can detect it (see Figure 38). To nontasters, PTC tastes just like paper. Determine the number of tasters and nontasters in your school. You can expand your project to

FIGURE 38. IF YOU'RE A TASTER, YOU'LL FIND
THAT PTC PAPER HAS A BITTER TASTE.

include your town's population; if you do, first check the bibliography for a reference on sampling techniques to be sure that you get a valid cross section of people.

You can include other human traits in your project on evolution: attached and free earlobes, ability to roll the tongue, hitchhiker's thumb, middigital hair, widow's peak, and crossed thumbs. Most biology textbooks will explain what to look for in each of these traits. An ambitious project would be to sample a sizable population for each of these traits and then analyze their evolutionary pattern using the Hardy-Weinberg principle. You may want to expand your project to compare how each trait is evolving in two populations that are geographically separated: a school in another town or a population in another state. Explain any differences you discover.

Some interesting discoveries about evolutionary patterns have been made by examining small, isolated populations. Examples include the Amish in Pennsylvania and Hassidic Jews. In both groups, these people form a tightly knit community, marrying within the population. This close interbreeding has caused genes to be far from equilibrium. If you know of a similar population, select a trait for analysis. Apply the Hardy-Weinberg principle to gauge its evolutionary progress.

You can use the Hardy-Weinberg principle for a project aimed at assessing the evolution of a trait in any animal or plant population consisting of more than five individuals. However, be aware of potential problems. The mathematics involved will be much simpler if the trait is the result of only two genetic factors. Many hereditary characteristics are the product of many genes working together. In such cases, calculations involving the Hardy-Weinberg principle will be difficult, if not impossible. If you undertake this type of project, select an organism genetically suited like *Drosophila*: easy to breed, fast generation time, and numerous progeny.

NATURAL SELECTION

If you discover that a particular genetic type in a population exceeds the amount expected according to the

Hardy-Weinberg principle, you can conclude that natural selection favors that group. As you may recall, organisms heterozygous for a trait are sometimes favored. The best-studied example involves sickle-cell anemia, a disease often proving fatal before a person reaches reproductive age. Consequently, the frequency of the gene causing this disease should gradually decline; this gene might even eventually disappear from the population.

Scientists were at first surprised to find this gene in many regions of Africa at a much higher frequency than they expected based on the Hardy-Weinberg principle. Upon investigating, they discovered that homozygous recessives were likely to get sickle-cell anemia, while homozygous dominants were likely to contract malaria. Those who were heterozygous were protected against both diseases. Since they carried the gene for this disease, they continued to pass it on to future generations.

Design a project to investigate the selection pressure exerted by the environment on different types of organisms within a population. Once again, *Drosophila* would be most suitable. Obtain flies with various wing patterns, eye colors, or body shapes. Place the same number of each type in identical vials. For example, put 10 males and 10 females with normal wings in one vial, 10 males and 10 females with curly wings in a second vial, and so on. Count how many offspring are produced in each case. Another procedure would involve taking the larvae from each type of fly and placing equal numbers in different vials. Record the number of adults that eventually hatch.

Experiment with changing the temperature, day-night cycle, and composition of the culture media. Determine whether the same genetic type is favored in every situation. Repeat your studies by mixing two or three different types in the same vial. For example, place flies with normal wings with an equal number of ones having curly wings in the same vial. Record which type produces the most offspring or hatches most successfully. Again, manipulate the environment to see if one type shows a greater survival rate under different environmental conditions.

Don't be surprised to discover that one type survives better in one situation, while another thrives under different circumstances. This is what biologists discovered when they studied a population of peppered moths that consisted mostly of light-colored moths. Some dark-colored moths were also present. However, scientists found that the dark-colored moths were becoming more abundant than the light forms in certain areas of England.

The trees in these regions were slowly becoming covered with soot and smoke from factories that sprung up during the Industrial Revolution in the late 18th century. Once rare, the dark moths now had an advantage in polluted areas since they blended in with their background and could not be easily seen by their predators. In non-polluted areas, the light-colored moths still had the advantage since birds could more easily find and eat the darker forms on the lighter trees (see Figure 39).

Carry out a project to see what happens as you gradually change the environment. Collect a population of insects and prepare a suitable chamber where they can live and reproduce. Once your population is thriving, add a small amount of insecticide to the chamber. Record the percentage of insects that survive. Allow these insects to repopulate the chamber, and then add the same amount of insecticide. Count your survivors and keep repeating the procedure. Graph your results and explain what happened to the percentage of survivors each time the insecticide was added.

Experiment with different insecticide concentrations. Explore what happens to your insect population if you use repeated exposures to one insecticide followed by a different insecticide. See if one insecticide has the same effect on different types of insects. You may turn up some interesting findings that have practical application. When the insecticide DDT was first used on houseflies, it killed most of them. Today, DDT is almost useless against houseflies. If your insect population follows the

Figure 39. Natural selection has favored the evolution of dark-colored moths in areas where soot has covered the bark of trees. Blending with their background, these moths are not easily seen by predator birds.

same pattern, perhaps you can uncover some way of preventing this increased resistance.

If you prefer to work with something other than insects, explore what happens to a bacterial population as you expose it to repeated doses of an antibiotic. Again, your project may have practical significance, since many bacterial populations have evolved so that most of the organisms are resistant to certain drugs. Penicillin, once highly effective against most bacteria, is useless at times in treating some types of bacterial infections. By combining recombinant DNA technology with a study of a bacterial population, you may find a method to slow down the evolution of resistant organisms.

Besides insects and bacteria, any animal or plant would be suitable to use in a project exploring the effects of a changing environment. But first you must identify some factor that is lethal to the organism under study, perhaps a poisonous chemical or particular level of ultraviolet radiation. Then set up your project to see how the population evolves as you subject the organisms to repeated treatments. Experiment with ways to alter how the population responds.

MIMICRY
AND
TAXONOMY

Obviously, a population does not exist by itself in nature. Any one location may contain hundreds or even thousands of different populations, all exposed to the same natural selection forces. In some cases, strong selection pressures may cause two or more species to evolve along a similar path. The result may be two species that strongly resemble one another. Whenever two different species bear striking resemblances, evolution has resulted in mimicry.

The best known example of mimicry involves two species of butterflies: monarchs and viceroys. A blue jay that has never before tasted a monarch will try to eat one. But the bird will soon find the monarch so distasteful that it spits it out. After several attempts at eating a monarch, the blue jay will not touch a viceroy. Viceroys look much like monarchs but are not distasteful. A blue jay that has not tasted a monarch will devour viceroys. But an experienced blue jay often refuses to eat either butterfly. The viceroy, looking much like a monarch, is often saved because of mimicry.

Select two organisms resembling each other but belonging to different species. See if mimicry has evolved as a protective mechanism by determining if only one species serves as prey. If you cannot locate mimics to use, make your own. For example, get some worms that birds find tasty and edible. Divide your worms into three groups. Make one distasteful by dipping them into a solution of quinine which is bitter. Mark them with a band of green paint. Take the second group, dip them in distilled water, and mark them with the same green color band. Dip the third group in distilled water, but mark them with an orange band of paint.

Feed equal numbers of the first and third groups to birds. Record what happens. After a pattern is established, introduce worms from all three groups. Determine if the second group is a successful mimic. Replace the third group with pipe cleaners colored and painted to look like the orange-banded worms. Experiment with different colors and paint patterns. Divide your worms into three groups using a method other than paint to distinguish between them. Establish the minimum amount of resemblance necessary to provide protection for a mimic. Find out if birds that have been starved for a few days respond the same way as ones that have been recently fed.

In some cases, mimics look so much alike that you might think they belong to the same species. In fact, biologists first classified organisms strictly on the basis of their appearance. The more closely they resembled each other, the more closely they were classified. However, biologists soon discovered that appearances could be deceiving (see Figure 40). Today, biologists depend on factors other than appearance: similarities in biochemistry, and particularly the ability to mate and produce fertile offspring. By definition, whenever two organisms reproduce fertile offspring, they are members of the same species.

Biologists are still unsure of the classification of many organisms, including both plants and animals. Contact a biologist who specializes in taxonomy, the classification

FIGURE 40. ALTHOUGH THE TARANTULA AND THE HORSESHOE CRAB DO NOT RESEMBLE EACH OTHER, THEY ARE CLOSELY RELATED. IN FACT, HORSESHOE CRABS ARE NOT CLASSIFIED WITH CRABS BUT ARE GROUPED WITH SPIDERS SUCH AS THE TARANTULA.

of organisms, for specific cases where questions exist. Conduct a project to see if you can determine if they belong to the same or different species. In some situations, taxonomists even argue whether one species should be divided into two separate ones. Perhaps your project might reveal the existence of two species, one of which might be named after you!

BIBLIOGRAPHY

The following books provide information on laboratory techniques or experiments that may spark additional ideas for biology projects.

Abramoff, Peter, and Robert G. Thomson. *Laboratory Outlines in Biology IV*. San Francisco: W. H. Freeman, 1986.

Beller, Joel. *Experimenting With Plants*. New York: Arco, 1985.

Benson, Harold J. *Microbiological Applications: Laboratory Manual in General Microbiology*. Dubuque, Iowa: Wm. C. Brown, 1985.

Biological Sciences Curriculum Study. *Research Problems in Biology*. 3 vols. New York: Oxford University Press, 1976.

Brown, Vinson. *Building Your Own Nature Museum for Study and Pleasure*. New York: Arco, 1985.

Gardner, Robert. *Ideas for Science Projects*. New York: Franklin Watts, 1986.

Heidemann, Merle K. *Exercises in Biological Sciences*. Belmont, Calif.: Wadsworth, 1984.

Johnson, Leland G. *Patterns and Experiments in Developmental Biology.* Dubuque, Iowa: Wm. C. Brown, 1973.

Winchester, A.M. *Laboratory Manual of Genetics.* Dubuque, Iowa: Wm. C. Brown, 1979.

Witham, Francis H., David F. Blaydes, and Robert E. Devlin. *Exercises in Plant Physiology.* Belmont, Calif.: Wadsworth, 1985.

The following books contain information on biochemistry, including techniques used in chromatography and electrophoresis.

Baum, Stuart, et al. *Exercises in Organic and Biological Chemistry.* New York: Macmillan, 1981.

Berman, William. *Beginning Biochemistry.* New York: Arco, 1968.

Clark, John M., and Robert L. Switzer. *Experimental Biochemistry.* San Francisco: W. H. Freeman, 1977.

Crandall, G. Douglas. *Selected Exercises for the Biochemistry Laboratory.* New York: Oxford University Press, 1983.

Gaal, O., et al. *Electrophoresis in the Separation of Biological Macromolecules.* New York: Wiley, 1980.

Lowman, Robert G., et al. *Experimental Introductory Chemistry: Organic and Biochemistry.* Washington, D.C.: American Press, 1983.

Simpson, Colin F. and Mary Whittaker. *Electrophoretic Techniques.* New York: Academic Press, 1983.

Strong, C. L. *The Amateur Scientist.* New York: Scientific American, 1961.

Strong, F. M., and Gilbert H. Koch. *Biochemistry Laboratory Manual.* Dubuque, Iowa: Wm. C. Brown, 1981.

The following books contain information on statistics, including information on the Hardy-Weinberg principle.

Bradley, Jack I., and James N. McClelland. *Basic Statistical Concepts: A Self-Instructional Text.* Glenview, Ill.: Scott, Foresman, 1978.

Campbell, R. C. *Statistics for Biologists.* New York: Cambridge University Press, 1967.

Curtis, Helena. *Biology.* New York: Worth, 1983. (See pages 893–897 for an explanation of the Hardy-Weinberg principle.)

Down, Jack. *Basic Statistics for High School.* East Lansing, Mich.: Golden Poplar Press, 1985.

Freund, John E. *Statistics: A First Course.* Englewood Cliffs, N.J.: Prentice-Hall, 1981.

The following books contain information on plants.

Davis, William K. *Laboratory Exercises for General Botany.* Washington, D.C.: American Press, 1981.

Devlin, Robert, and Francis Witham. *Plant Physiology.* Belmont, Calif.: Wadsworth, 1983.

Stern, Kingsley R. *Introductory Plant Biology.* Dubuque, Iowa: Wm. C. Brown, 1985.

The following books contain information you will need if you plan to enter your biology project in a science fair.

Beller, Joel. *So You Want to Do a Science Project!* New York: Arco, 1982.

Smith, Norman F. *How Fast Do Your Oysters Grow?* New York: Julian Messner, 1982.

Tocci, Salvatore. *How to Do a Science Fair Project.* New York: Franklin Watts, 1986.

Van Deman, Barry A., and Ed McDonald. *Nuts and Bolts: A Matter Of Fact Guide For Science Fair Projects.* Harwood Heights, Ill.: The Science Man Press, 1985.

INDEX

ABOUT THE AUTHOR

Salvatore Tocci teaches biology and chemistry at East Hampton High School on Long Island, New York, where he is chairman of the science department. He has written educational software and audiovisual programs and has given workshops at conventions for science teachers. Mr. Tocci is also the author of *Chemistry Around You: Experiments and Projects with Everyday Products* and *How to Do a Science Fair Project,* the latter published by Franklin Watts. He and his family live in East Hampton, New York.